The Use of York:
Characteristics of the Medieval Liturgical Office in York

by

Matthew Cheung Salisbury
Worcester College
Oxford University

BORTHWICK PAPER NO. 113

First Published 2008

© Matthew Cheung Salisbury

ISSN: 0524-0913
ISBN-13: 978-1-904497-25-7

Acknowledgements

I am particularly grateful for the advice of Dr Cristina Dondi and Professor Richard Sharpe.

The Arundel Antiphonal appears by permission of Lady Herries of Terregles and the Trustees of the Arundel Castle Archives. I am grateful to the several libraries and archives that made their manuscript collections available, and wish particularly to thank for their assistance Dr Dorothy Johnston of the University of Nottingham; Dr John Robinson and Mrs Sara Rodger of Arundel Castle; and Mr Peter Young, Archivist of York Minster. In Oxford, Duke Humfrey was an ideal base of operations, and I thank the staff for their help. Finally, I thank Professor Nigel Morgan for generously allowing me to consult unpublished material and for supplying helpful advice.

The Social Sciences and Humanities Research Council of Canada, Trinity College, Toronto, and the Edward Kylie Trust are to be thanked for their generous financial support.

Professor Andrew Hughes, among his manifold kindnesses, provoked an enduring need to explore 'general impressions', and made preoccupation with such explorations acceptable.

St Everild's Day, 2008.

Abbreviations

Manuscripts to which frequent references are made
Full details of all manuscripts are in the first part of the Bibliography.

Arundel	Arundel Castle Archives	York Antiphonal (s.n.)
BLAdd.30511	London, British Library	ms Additional 30511
BLAdd.34190	"	mss Additional 34190 & Egerton 2025
BLAdd.38624	"	ms Additional 38624
Burney.335	"	ms Burney 335
CAdd.2602	Cambridge, University Library	ms Additional 2602
CAdd.3110	"	ms Additional 3110
Cosin	Durham, University Library	ms Cosin V.I.2
Gough.lit.1	Oxford, Bodleian Library	ms Gough liturg. 1
Gough.lit.5	"	ms Gough liturg. 5
Harley.2785	London, British Library	ms Harley 2785
Lat.liturg.f.2	Oxford, Bodleian Library	ms Lat. liturg. F.2
Laud.misc.84	"	ms Laud misc. 84
Laud.misc.299	"	ms Laud misc. 299
Rawl.C.553	"	ms Rawlinson C. 553
Rawl.G.170	"	ms Rawlinson G. 170
Sion	London, Lambeth Palace Library	ms Sion College 1
Wollaton	Nottingham, University Library	the Wollaton Antiphonal (s.n.)
Wood.C.12	Oxford, Bodleian Library	ms Wood C. 12
XVI.O.9	York, Minster Archives	ms XVI O. 9
XVI.O.23	"	ms XVI O. 23
YAdd.68	"	ms Additional 68
YAdd.69	"	ms Additional 69
YAdd.70	"	ms Additional 70
YAdd.115	"	ms Additional 115
YAdd.383	"	ms Additional 383

Reference works

CAO	Hesbert, *Corpus Antiphonalium Officii*
LCS	Bradshaw, ed., *Lincoln Cathedral Statutes*
MMBL	Ker, ed., *Medieval Manuscripts in British Libraries*
van Dijk	*Handlist of the Latin Liturgical Manuscripts in the Bodleian*

Liturgical items are often referred to in the following format: **A3 MR3.8g** = the third responsory, in mode 8 beginning on G, of Matins for the third Sunday in Advent

A1, 2, 3, 4	First through fourth Sundays in Advent
Thu, Fri, Sat	Maundy Thursday, Good Friday, Holy Saturday
ML, MR, MV	Matins lesson, responsory, or verse; accompanied by a number indicating the order of the item

The Use of York:
Characteristics of the Medieval Liturgical Office in York

- 1 -

Describing the Use of York: A new agenda for an unsolved problem

The state of liturgy in Britain before the Prayer Book is often described in the words of the well-known Preface:

> And whereas heretofore there hath bene great diversitie in saying & synging in Churches within this realme; some folowing Salisbury use, some Herford use, some the use of Bangor, some of yorke, some of Lincoln; now from henceforth all the whole realm shal have but one use.[1]

The passage implies the continued existence of established local rites, although the author may have overstated their diversity. It has long been accepted that in later medieval England the use of Sarum, which had developed from the customs of Salisbury Cathedral, eventually superseded most of the other local patterns. At least one significant regional use did remain at the English Reformation: that of York, a counterpart to Sarum used throughout the northern province. The origins and survival of the use of York in spite of the ascendancy of Sarum demand explanation. But in order to discuss such matters it is necessary first to determine what was meant by York use and to consider the properties by which York liturgy differed from the dominant pattern.

It has not been possible to carry out such work since the distinguishing characteristics of York use, and indeed those of Sarum use, have suffered from a lack of attention and consequently a lack of definition. Although the *idea* of a use seems well understood, at least by the frequency of its application, those who have worked most closely with the sources have pointed out that the parameters of specific uses remain largely undefined. The late David Chadd observed that despite the number of extant Sarum sources the wider context of the use remains unclear.[2] Nigel Morgan has pointed out that the dearth of recent work on Sarum has meant that modern scholars now rely on editions produced over a hundred years ago which contain 'misinterpretations' on the part of the editors.[3] Work seems to have stalled on the analysis of the Sarum use — perhaps because the task is so challenging — but it continues to be a point of reference for many who cite it, unaware of these ongoing problems of definition.

The situation is even worse for York. To date, nearly all scholarly works involving York use have referred to the liturgy presented in editions produced for the Surtees Society at the end of the nineteenth century. These are the only modern texts of the York pattern that are available; but to Richard Pfaff, they 'leave something to be desired by late twentieth-century standards'.[4] In the case of the office, with which this paper will be concerned, the edition produced by the Revd Stephen Lawley in 1880 is a transcription, more or less, of the first printed breviary of York, produced in 1493.[5] References in Ker's *Medieval Manuscripts in British Libraries*, then, to some breviary with 'deviation in its lections from *Brev. Ebor*'[6], indicate only that the text in the manuscript deviates from the text of a single printed edition. Reliance on this edition is far from rare.[7]

Little if any serious work has been done with the manuscripts of the York office, beyond elementary descriptions for catalogues. Such catalogues, too, suffer, because assignments to York have so far been based on deficient methods: first, a reliance on comparison with the unrepresentative edition; second, and more importantly, the assumption that certain entries in a liturgical calendar are peculiar to a given use, within which all calendars are more or less consistent. A combination of these questionable methods has meant that a number of manuscripts have been mistakenly assigned to York, and their several properties confused with those of the sources more reliably assigned to the use. The unique characteristics of the York tradition, then, not to mention any insights about its origins or longevity, or how properly to identify it by recognizing such properties, remain unknown.

A first step towards a more definitive discussion of York use must be to identify the liturgical features that were characteristic of its sources. This paper attempts, through the first comparative analysis of York office manuscripts, to identify those features by framing and applying a set of methodological techniques that are effective for such work. Based on the most telling characteristics of the use, it will be possible to make some suggestions about its origins and its relationship with Sarum.

In the course of this study, it will be necessary first to re-assess the manuscripts presently associated with York. An established method of comparing liturgical patterns will eliminate a number of manuscripts whose connexion to York is tenuous. With the remaining sources, identified as a coherent group validly assigned to York, we shall compare liturgical contents to determine what distinctive properties they share, which, with some reservations, we shall accept as characteristics of the use. The result is more complex than that provided by a simple comparison with the printed breviary: while certain aspects of the use are uniform, others diverge in different ways in every manuscript; still others are linked to Sarum. All indications point to a more varied use of York, obscured by simplistic reliance on the 1493 breviary, and suggest complex relations between York and the other regional English liturgies.

* * *

Much editorial and comparative work dealing with medieval liturgy, including the use of York, needs to be treated with caution, and some of it should be disregarded entirely. Studies tend to eschew manuscripts and to rely heavily on editions of English service books from the several main uses, many of which were produced as historical models for Church of England ritual or to prove the relation of late medieval English liturgy to Anglo-Saxon and Roman patterns.[8] Liturgical scholarship has often been concerned with tracing the history of modern rites back to antiquity; Paul Bradshaw has written that some have even 'tried to arrange the evidence so as to suggest that a single coherent line of liturgical evolution can be traced from the apostolic age'.[9] The resulting volumes have never fallen out of favour, perhaps owing to a reluctance to do more work when the rites had apparently been so clearly described in print. Yet a number are deficient; some, like the Surtees edition of the York breviary and its well-known Sarum counterpart edited by Procter and Wordsworth, were simply transcribed from a single source of no particular authority by their editors' own admission. The editors of the latter believed that a transcription was a 'more manageable undertaking' but did look forward to a critical edition in the future,[10] a task whose eventual necessity was quickly forgotten, perhaps because of the convenience of the existing version. Many editors of liturgical texts were clerics of the Church of England with antiquarian interests, and

Pfaff notes that their work was invariably coloured by 'the presuppositions of those who worship according to printed liturgical books' i.e., the assumption that liturgical books of a certain pattern, whatever their age or provenance, ought not to vary.[11] The preference, then, for the single printed edition as an exemplar for the Surtees volume, rather than multiple manuscripts, may have been dictated not so much by mere laziness as by an assumption that it was an accurate representation of the York liturgy, manuscript or otherwise, in the year 1493. The term used by these scholars to describe their own work — 'liturgiology' — is useful to compartmentalize such studies. [12]

The school of liturgiology is not dead. A more recent work by Philip Baxter with a promising title summarizes the familiar scholarship on the descent of Roman forms to Britain, speaking approvingly of a 'drastic and efficient Norman reorganization', and a Sarum use that 'gained increasing value as an authoritative reference and source of proven ... liturgy'.[13] Perhaps Baxter's most perceptive observation is that Sarum was 'taken up again [in the 19th century] by churches of the Anglo-Catholic party'.[14] The editors of a retrospective on the work of Walter Howard Frere describe some of the difficulties of liturgiology and neatly summarize some of its problems: it is a field 'where the power of convention and the queer desire for "mumbo jumbo" are apt to be all powerful'.[15]

Liturgical research has not, of course, been restricted to observations defined by presumption or piety. The present study relies on methodological principles, successfully applied by several modern scholars, which are reliant on the amassing of quantitative data. An important work by Anton Baumstark, *Comparative Liturgy*, forbade the researcher to 'accept any preconceived ideas' and argued, as if speaking directly to liturgiologists, that:

> the history of Liturgy occupies [a position] in the totality
> of the sciences ... it is only by setting out from exact results
> and precise observations that right conclusions will be reached.
> The scrupulous establishment of the factual data underlying the
> problems should precede every attempt at explanation.[16]

The 'establishment of the factual data' in immense quantities was an essential element of liturgical research in the second half of the twentieth century. Among the most prominent contributions was the six-volume *Corpus antiphonalium officii* of René-Jean Hesbert, a work that supplied partial contents of 798 manuscripts and attempted to trace the descent of the distinctive

patterns they contained.[17] Hesbert collected series of Matins responsories and
verses with the intention of producing, through comparison by shared variant,
a 'restitution critique de l'Archetype de la tradition'.[18] Though his objective
is now deprecated, Hesbert's methods for collecting and comparing data, and
the corpus he produced, remain useful means by which an unknown source
can be compared with a great many others. Based on the contents of twelve
manuscripts, Hesbert edited the responsory texts for Sundays in Advent and
assigned a unique number to each text. It was then possible to draw up a
'responsory series' for a manuscript by collating the numbers corresponding
to each of the nine responsories for each Sunday in Advent. These series could
then be compared by hand or by computer, and relations between sources
highlighted. The *CAO* corpus is now 'the best-known tool for supra-regional
comparisons'.[19] In similar fashion, responsory series for the Triduum were first
collected by Raymond le Roux and reorganized by Pierre-Marie Gy.[20] Gabriel
Beyssac collected some 1275 responsory series for the office for the Dead
from manuscripts across Europe, and claimed to have been able to identify
the liturgical tradition of a manuscript solely from its responsory series for the
Dead.[21] His work was supplemented by Victor Leroquais, Pierre-Marie Gy,
and Michel Huglo, and computerized and studied in depth by Knud Ottosen.[22]
The present study utilizes the method refined by all of these scholars, and it
will be shown that the responsory series that they have associated with York
are valid indicators of the use.

Rather than beginning with an historical supposition (e.g., that Anglo-Saxon
liturgy was linked to Rome) and determining the parameters for study of the
sources based on that premise, liturgical research in the later twentieth century
became focused on first collecting the contents of the sources before proposing
any reasons for the trends observed. I speculate that this preoccupation with
data may have convinced some researchers that the presence of some given
element, for instance a feastday associated with a certain region, could be an
indicator of use.

Janet Backhouse's edition of the Madresfield Hours illustrates the most
popular means for assignment to York use, the presence of the feasts of certain
saints associated with York in the calendar: generally these are Paulinus of York
(10 October; d. 644), Wilfrid of Ripon (12 October; d. 709), John of Beverley
(7 May, transl. 25 October; d. 721), and William of York (8 June; d. 1154).
For Backhouse, their presence suggests that 'the York connection is ... in no
doubt'.[23] Van Dijk's catalogue of liturgical manuscripts in the Bodleian also

relies on the contents of calendars to assign a book to a use, but seems less likely to trust evidence without question. My recent collaborations with Andrew Hughes have also considered evidence from calendars to assign manuscripts of unknown use to York.[24] Nigel Morgan's database of liturgical books is also based partly on evidence from calendars.[25]

But calendars were functional — indeed many were the most well-thumbed leaves in a manuscript — and easy to modify, and their contents may therefore not reflect the original contents, or indeed the surviving contents, of the rest of the book. In this study, it will be established that most calendar entries common in York books are not found exclusively in sources of that use. Summary assignments, particularly to York, based solely on the presence or absence of such a small set of items must now be distrusted, and a wider range of liturgical contents must be consulted.

- 2 -
Liturgical Analysis

Given several existing lists of manuscripts assigned to York, Hesbert's method of summarizing liturgical contents has been adopted here in order to assess the validity of each assignment. Based on their responsory series, certain of these manuscripts were found to contain distinctive patterns associated by *CAO* and related works (those of le Roux, Gy, and Beyssac) with York; these sources will be deemed the 'York group'.

Other manuscripts from the existing lists contain some material, mostly calendar entries, that might be associated with York, but their responsory series follow the Sarum pattern. These manuscripts were not selected as representative Sarum sources; indeed, they might be better categorized as 'York rejects'. However, they are associated with Sarum just as securely as their counterparts are associated with York: both groups contain the responsory series established by *CAO* as unique to each use.

To determine the common features of the York manuscripts, several aspects of each source will be studied, beginning with the calendar, moving to the Sanctorale and Litany, and ending with an analysis of a number of plainsong melodies. Where manuscripts are incomplete or damaged, and where their contents may be difficult to interpret or even contradictory, it will be shown that data derived from several components of a manuscript will help to support conclusions. Broadly, we will move from what is understood — the summary assignment of certain manuscripts to a certain tradition — to what is unknown, that is, the properties of that tradition which ought to underpin such an assignment.

Lists of presumed York office manuscripts can be found in the Surtees editions, and are summarized and supplemented in Frere's 1927 tract *York Service Books*.[26] I know of no lists of manuscripts linked to York that have been published recently, and I am grateful to Nigel Morgan and Andrew Hughes for sharing their unpublished lists. The following table sets out a comparison of the several lists of office books that have been assigned to York use, in addition to a list derived from van Dijk's catalogue of liturgical books.[27]

It was felt that expert reappraisal of the evidence would be necessary if estimates of the dates of these manuscripts were to be given. For the present purpose it ought to be sufficient to state, based on the consensus from existing catalogues, that all of the sources studied were written in either the fourteenth or fifteenth century, like many extant English liturgical books.

It was not possible to see all of the manuscripts during the course of the present work. The two manuscripts in Dublin, the Leeds fragment, and the two breviaries in America await attention at a later date, and they do not appear further in this study. Two others have been seen but are omitted: BLAdd.28598 was studied closely by Diane Droste[28] who does not accept an assignment to York, and BLAdd.37511 contains no Matins services. It should be noted that only one of the surviving sources used at St Mary's Abbey, York (Bodleian Rawlinson C.553), has been studied. This manuscript follows a secular order of service; usually monastic manuscripts followed different liturgical patterns; these will require investigation at a later date. Only one source with a monastic order of service (the Burney manuscript) appears in the lists; at present we will consider only the secular sources of the York office, which contain the characteristic responsory series.

Responsories, verses, and lessons

Hesbert's method of comparison by responsory series may not immediately appear to be useful for English sources, perhaps because the several regional liturgical patterns of medieval England do not appear to have varied as greatly as those in Continental sources; where neighbouring cities employed conspicuously different local uses.[29] But the technique is effective; first, because

Manuscript	Frere	Morgan	Hughes	van Dijk (Bodleian books only)	this study
Arundel Castle York Antiphonal (for York Collegiate Chapel of St Mary & Holy Angels)	X (Everingham, Lord Herries)	X (2 entries: Arundel Castle; Everingham)	X (2 entries: Arundel Castle; Everingham)		X
Cambridge Add. 2602 (for Springfield, Essex)			X		X (Sarum)
Cambridge Add. 3110	X	X	X		X
Durham Cosin V. I. 2 (for Rudby)	X	X	X		X
BL Add. 28598			X		seen (Ely?)
BL Add. 30511		X	X		X
BL Add. 34190	X	X	X		X (see Egerton 2025)
BL Add. 37511	X	X	X		seen, not used
BL Add. 38624		X	X		X
BL Burney 335 (Cistercian)	X		X		X (monastic)
BL Egerton 2025					X (see Add 34190)
BL Harley 2785			X		X (Sarum)
Lambeth Palace, Sion 1 olim Arc.L.40.2/L.1 (for Skelton)	X	X	X		X
Nott. Univ, Wollaton Antiphonal			X		X (Sarum)
Bodl. Gough lit.1	X (as Gough 36)	X	X	X	X
Bodl. Gough lit.5	X	X	X	X	X

Source				
Bodl. Lat. liturg.f.2			X	X (Sarum)
Bodl. Laud misc.84 (for York Minster?)	X	X	X	X
Bodl. Laud misc.299 (for Launton, Oxon)		X	X (Sarum)	X (Sarum)
Bodl. Rawl.C.553 (for St Mary's, York)			X	X (orig. Sarum)
Bodl. Rawl. G.170	X		X	X
Bodl. Wood C.12			X	X (Sarum)
York Minster XVI.O.9	X	X		X
York Minster XVI.O.23		X		X
York Minster Add.68	X	X		X
York Minster Add.69 (for Brandesburton)		X		X
York Minster Add.70 (for Harewood)		X	X	X
York Minster Add.115		X		X
York Minster Add.383		X		X
Trinity Coll Dublin, B.3.9(85)	X	X		not seen
Trinity Coll Dublin, B.3.11(87)	X	X		not seen
Leeds Univ, Ripon 8		X		not seen
Urbana Univ, ms 130		X		not seen
Grolier Club ms 3		X		not seen

Table 1 – Lists of presumed York office books; X indicates the presence of the source.

it is useful to note the great consistency within manuscripts of a certain group; and second, because this uniformity is made even more significant when comparison shows that no known Western liturgical tradition shares the exact series in question. *CAO* supplies normative Advent responsory series for Sarum and York, the latter based on a consistent pattern in five sources: these were Arundel (labelled Everingham); Trinity College Dublin mss 85 and 87; Sion (giving the Sion College shelfmark); and York Minster XVI.O.9.[30]

In addition to series from the four Sundays and three quarter days in Advent, I considered responsory series from Matins during the Triduum (Maundy Thursday, Good Friday, and Holy Saturday); and Matins of the Dead (2 November, but also found as a freestanding devotional office). On the suggestion of Cristina Dondi, who has made use of unpublished work by Pierre-Marie Gy, I included Matins of All Saints (1 November).

Every secular manuscript from our list that contains responsories (some, by design, do not) follows either the York or the Sarum series as reported in *CAO* and its supplements,[31] which allows us to divide the manuscripts into two distinct groups. York responsory series were found in seventeen manuscripts and in the 1493 printed breviary: six manuscripts and the edition contained every service; five had partial contents owing to damage or missing leaves; and six, by design, contained only certain services, in most cases the office of the Dead.

Seven manuscripts from the lists of books associated with York had the series associated with Sarum, of which two were complete, and four contained only the office of the Dead. The York and Sarum manuscripts are summarized in the list below.

	Sources aligning with York series; the 'York group'	Sources aligning with Sarum series; the 'Sarum group'
complete	1493; Arundel; Sion; Laud. misc.84; XVI.O.9; YAdd.68; YAdd.70	CAdd.2602; Laud.misc.299
incomplete	CAdd.3110; BLAdd.30511; BLAdd.34190/Egerton.2025; BLAdd 38624; Gough.lit.1; Gough.lit.5; Rawl.G.170; XVI.O.23; YAdd.69; YAdd.115; YAdd.383	Harley.2785; Lat.liturg.F.2; Wollaton; Rawl.C.553[32]; Wood.C.12

	1493 series	York series	Sarum series
MR1	Credo quod redemptor V. Quem visurus sum	Credo quod redemptor V. Quem visurus sum	Credo quod redemptor V. Quem visurus sum
MR2	Qui lazarum resuscitasti **V. Requiem eternam**	Qui lazarum resuscitasti **V. Requiem eternam**	Qui lazarum resuscitasti **V. Qui venturus es**
MR3	Domine quando veneris V. Commissa mea pavesco	Domine quando veneris V. Commissa mea pavesco	Domine quando veneris V. Commissa mea pavesco
MR4	Heu mihi domine V. Anima mea turbata est	Heu mihi domine V. Anima mea turbata est	Heu mihi domine V. Anima mea turbata est
MR5	Ne recorderis peccata mea V. Dirige domine	Ne recorderis peccata mea V. Dirige domine	Ne recorderis peccata mea V. Dirige domine deus
MR6	**Libera me domine** **V. Clamantes et dicentes**	**Libera me domine** **V. Clamantes et dicentes**	Domine secundum actum meum **V. Amplius lava me**
MR7	Peccantem me cotidie **V. Deus in nomine**	Peccantem me cotidie V. Deus in nomine	Peccantem me cotidie V. Deus in nomine
MR8	**Deus eterne in cuius** **V. Qui in cruce positus**	**Deus eterne in cuius** **V. Qui in cruce positus**	**Requiem eternam dona eis** **V. Qui lazarum resuscitasti**
MR9	Libera me domine de morte eterna V. Dies illa dies irae	Libera me domine de morte eterna V. Dies illa dies irae	Libera me domine de morte eterna V. Dies illa dies irae

Table 2 - example responsory series for the office of the Dead showing differences between Sarum and York orders as defined by CAO, and the series in the 1493 breviary (identical with the CAO York series). Compare the inconsistent lessons in table 3.

Both the York and Sarum groups are defined by their respective responsory series for Advent, the Triduum, All Saints, and the Dead: each manuscript in a group, so far as it is complete, contains the same characteristic series. Other sources in the lists above do not contain any responsory series and cannot be assigned, although their features are discussed elsewhere in this study. As for the Sarum manuscripts, all properly 'rejects' from York use, the reader will accept that despite the unpremeditated method of their selection, in the absence of similarly detailed work for Sarum and given their uniformity with the established series these manuscripts will constitute for us a putative 'Sarum group'. [33]

The question may fairly be raised why manuscripts which have been associated with York should have Sarum responsory series. In the case of each manuscript in our Sarum group, the former assignment to York was evidently made based on other criteria, particularly the presence of the 'York saints'. The Wollaton Antiphonal calendar, for example, contains the feasts of Wilfrid, William, and John of Beverley, but the responsory series in this manuscript follow the Sarum pattern. Since the feasts in question were added in a distinctive hand, and none of the saints' feasts appear elsewhere in the book, an assignment to York must be dismissed. Laud misc.299, similarly, contains a considerable amount of material for John of Beverley; this likewise has been added to the original contents of the book, most likely after the widespread adoption of John's cult in or after the early fifteenth century.

I have attempted to contribute a new element to this comparative work by transcribing *incipits* of the accompanying lessons. A representative set, lessons for the Triduum, is supplied in Table 3. A brief glimpse at each lesson (the first three words) is enough to identify the text, and series of these incipits are sufficient to determine, on a basic level, whether sources that share responsory series also share their lessons. The lessons studied thus far indicate that there was considerably less uniformity within the manuscripts of the York tradition than the stability of their series might otherwise indicate.

The first three words of each lesson in the Matins services studied were transcribed from the eleven York manuscripts that contained lessons; even within this small set, considerable variation was evident. For instance, while the first lesson of Sunday of Advent 1 — *visio ysaiae filii*[34] — is the same in every manuscript and in the 1493 breviary, the texts of the next two lessons do not agree in any more than four sources, and no manuscript has the lessons that appear in 1493. Lesson 4, however, appears uniformly as *leticia quanta sit* in all but one manuscript, XVI.O.9.

The lessons for Advent and the Triduum are particularly variable: no two sources have the same set of texts; and while one lesson may be shared between two or more sources, that relation is no indication that any other material is shared by that particular group. But a few observations are possible if every lesson and every service are considered. On nine separate occasions a lesson text appears only in YAdd.69, YAdd.70, and Laud.misc.84.[32] A further seven lessons can be found only in the same three sources and Sion.[36] Another four are shared by Sion, YAdd.70, and Laud.misc.84.[37] A core group of YAdd.69, 70, and Laud.misc.84, then, share 16 items found nowhere else, of which 7 are shared by Sion.

Although YAdd.69 and YAdd.70 are both dated to the fifteenth century, on a superficial level they are not particularly similar. The former, a large noted breviary, has marginalia relating to *brandisborton* (Brandesburton), some 8 miles northeast of Beverley.[38] Based on obits and the dedication feast in the calendar, Ker inferred that the latter was produced for use in Harewood parish, just north of Leeds.[39]

Ker also noted that in both YAdd.69 and YAdd.70 there are inconsistencies between the lessons and those found in the printed breviary. The precise nature of these inconsistencies, along with those found in the rest of the manuscripts, can now be defined. In no single Matins service in Advent or the Triduum does the 1493 edition present more than five texts that appear as the relevant lesson in the majority of the manuscript sources. In most cases the edition concurs with the dominant manuscript tradition in two or three lessons within a given service of Matins, and does not for the remaining ones; most lessons in the manuscripts (in roman type, p. 52) never appear in the edition. Sometimes the edition's lesson is not found in any known manuscript. If quantitative proof is needed of the inconsistencies between the edition and the manuscript tradition, or indeed among the manuscripts themselves, the lessons in these two seasons undeniably supply it.

In contrast, the two services from the Sanctorale, All Saints and the Dead, have extremely consistent lessons. For All Saints, the edition agrees with the majority of manuscripts, and there are no more than two alternative texts per lesson. The lessons for the Dead are almost completely invariant; in contrast to Advent and the Triduum, they are identical with one exception (lesson 4) for both Sarum and York. Ottosen pointed out that the precise origin of the office for the Dead is uncertain, although some of the lessons, owing to their widespread popularity, must have been adopted at the 'oldest stage of the evolution of the Office', i.e. during the 9th and 10th centuries. Beyssac too concluded that although identification of a unique local responsory series for the Dead was a good diagnostic of use, the lessons were quite uniform.[40]

In this section, it has been demonstrated that responsory series enable a distinction to be drawn between the liturgical patterns of the Sarum and York uses. The inconsistency of Matins lessons in the York sources has also been illustrated. With the two groups in mind, each clearly defined by their responsory series, we will begin to survey other aspects of the books with a mind to identifying other distinctive contents that appear to be proper to York (or to Sarum) in the calendar and the Sanctorale.

The Calendar, Sanctorale, and Litany

We may often know exactly where a liturgical book was owned, but this may not mean that it represents the appropriate local use. Absent any explicit evidence of provenance from a manuscript,[41] and bearing in mind both that some liturgical patterns are broadly similar and that close textual comparison is tedious and not always productive, lists of saints in a liturgical manuscript have been treated as a short cut to uncovering where the book was used in worship and, by extension, assigning it to a use. But liturgical use and provenance must not be confused. Cults of some saints *can* be quite localized, and it is sometimes helpful to compare the saints that feature in an unprovenanced book with those in sources that can be assigned to a place of use on secure evidence; assignments of manuscripts to the use of York have been based on the appearance of four saints of Northern importance, Paulinus, Wilfrid, William, and John of Beverley. It is, however, necessary to determine whether these saints, or any others, are actually unique to the York liturgy before their presence can be treated as diagnostic.

Saints and their feastdays are prominent in at least three distinct sections of a liturgical book, but there is a tendency to focus only on the most accessible. The calendar seems to permit the avoidance of the Sanctorale, whose contents are often extensive and invariably less clear than those of the briefer, tabular calendar. It is also preferred to the Litany, for the latter tends to supply only an incomplete list of saints, some of whom are part of a standard formula and may not figure in the liturgical activities prescribed by the book.

Gathered in considerable numbers, transcriptions of calendars may reveal patterns of practice that permit the assignment of individual witnesses to a region or facilitate the analysis of widespread developments. Francis Wormald's collections of English Benedictine Calendars are well known.[42] Nigel Morgan has argued convincingly for a reassessment of the date of the widespread adoption of Sarum based on evidence from calendars.[43] They seem, then, particularly suitable for the present study of York manuscripts and their characteristics, though Frere, in his survey of the Victorian editions of the Sarum, York, and Hereford breviaries, described variations between their calendars as 'considerable in number, but not very great in importance'.[44] It ought to be pointed out, however, that he treated the calendars in the editions as though they represented practices that were uniform in their respective dioceses. Until the widespread adoption of consistent printed editions this must not have been the case.

Richard Pfaff has expressed reservations about the validity of calendars as expressions of actual practice at any given time or place. The appearance of a feast in a calendar, he proposes, may not necessarily indicate its observance, merely 'some degree of recognition'; and the date of the official promulgation of a feastday cannot be said always to align with the date of the introduction of that feast into a calendar.[45] Pfaff also criticizes Wormald's collections, whose effects were 'deleterious' since the transcriptions appear 'virtually without context'.[46] It is this last aspect that summarizes the principal problem: evidence from calendars is often considered in isolation, separate from other aspects of the surrounding manuscript.

In an effort to provide some of the context here, the manuscripts will be grouped according to their responsory series as previously defined. The manuscripts containing York responsory series ought to be associated most reliably with York, and their calendars ought to illustrate the patterns of practice, diverse or otherwise, that formed part of the York liturgy. Similarly, the Sarum group (also defined by responsory series) should supply its own proper patterns.

In many of the manuscripts additional material can be studied. First, we can compare the contents of the calendar with those of the Sanctorale. If the book was never modified, the two ought to agree, and if there are inconsistencies, they may suggest when and where a book was altered, and offer clues as to its places of use. In the absence of a calendar (and this is the case for Arundel, CAdd.3110, BLAdd.30511, BLAdd.38624, and Gough.lit.1) I have derived a listing of the saints in the manuscript from the Sanctorale. Second, another listing of the saints — the Litany — in the contents of liturgical books containing a Psalter will be considered.

Table 4 provides a summary of the 98 days of the year for which the calendars of the York group and the Sarum group supply different entries, and gives specific details for certain manuscripts. Each group presents a distinct set of feasts: twenty-seven feasts were found only in the Sarum group, and all of these were found in each of the three Sarum manuscripts surveyed. Thirty-nine feasts were found only in the York books, and seventeen of these were in every York manuscript. These feasts are listed at the end of the table.

Among the seventeen feasts peculiar to the York group, a number are for saints of local importance: William, Paulinus, and Wilfrid are obvious choices, along with Gilbert and Aidan.[47] It ought to be mentioned that these three of the four putative 'York saints' do appear in every book with a York responsory series. So too does John of Beverley, but his feastday and Translation also appear in several manuscripts in the Sarum group. As for St Everild, a nun associated with Wilfrid, it appears that the York use is the sole surviving source for her cult.[48] Other saints (Antony, Polycarp, Albinus, Urban, Austreberta) are not peculiar to York, but appear consistently in its calendar. The frequent appearance of Petroc, associated with the West Country, is notable.[49]

Tables containing the York calendar as edited by Henderson in the York Missal reveal that four of the saints that appear in every extant York office manuscript were not in the 12th-century copy of the calendar known to him.[50] These, unsurprisingly, were Gilbert of Sempringham (d. 1189), William of York (can. 1227, tr. 1283), King Edward the Confessor (can. 1161), and Martha (relics found c. 1187).

Mention must be made of the 22 other saints found in the York books that do not appear in every manuscript. Some of these (including Pelagia, Emerentiana, and Willibrord) appear in all but one source in the York group, while others appear in only a few. Conspicuous similarities in the calendar may suggest relations between manuscripts. Bede appears (alongside Augustine of Canterbury) in six books — Sion, Cosin, YAdd.68, 69, 70, and Laud.misc.84. Sion and Cosin share a further three uncommon saints: Chad with YAdd.383 and YAdd.69, and Sytha and Barbara with XVI.O.23. That these saints should appear only in these books suggests, at the least, that Sion and Cosin may be related. Other saints are conspicuously absent: Hilda, for instance, is missing from the Arundel and Sion books.

It is surely tempting to consider the seventeen feastdays found in every York manuscript, but not in the Sarum group, as easily identifiable hallmarks of the tradition. But while they may be characteristic of York use, they are by no means exclusive to it, even if they are not found in the Sarum calendars in the present study. It will be obvious that several of the seventeen key feasts — Antony and Urban, to give the most obvious examples — were observed across the Latin West, *including* the province of York, but do not appear in the Sarum sources we have considered. A random glance through Wormald's volumes[51] reveals five of the seventeen feastdays (Antony, Aidan, Grimbald, Paulinus, and Wilfrid), along with two others (Barbara and Botulph) in the calendar of Abingdon Abbey, which was neither in the province of York nor especially related to it. These saints are present for other reasons: Wormald explains the presence of Aidan, for instance, as a result of the association of Abingdon with Glastonbury, which claimed relics of Aidan,[52] and notes that Abingdon itself held a relic of Wilfrid. Abingdon is not the sole venue outside York to observe the feasts of 'York saints'; other examples exist, and much more work needs to be done in order to determine how widely these local saints were venerated outside York.[53]

One other calendar entry does appear to be unique to York: the feast of relics (19 October). It commemorates all of the saints whose relics were said to rest in the Minster,[54] among them those of William, and the texts for the day appropriately included several drawn from the Common of Saints. Everild's feastday and the *festum reliquiarum* are the only consistent York observances that, as far as I have been able to determine, were not in the calendar anywhere else.

It must be concluded that the presence or absence of feastdays in the calendar is still a dangerous means of assignment in isolation, and that the basis for arguing that a feast is peculiar to a given use is faulty — for such a feast may be unique within the set or sets considered, but it may not be so if other sources are taken into account. The producers of synoptic tables of the liturgical calendars of Sarum, York, and Hereford almost certainly suffered from this oversight.[55] It must be concluded that while the seventeen key feastdays are one eminent characteristic of all manuscripts *presently associated* with York, it is not possible to assign otherwise unassigned sources to York based on the presence or absence of such items.

We should therefore consider the remaining non-York manuscripts that have been associated with the use, and the cults of the saints whose feastdays have provoked their assignment. British Library Burney 335 is a fourteenth-century Cistercian breviary. Since it is complete, it includes responsory series for Advent, the Triduum, and the commemoration feasts, but the manuscript follows the monastic cursus. The series do not conform either to the Sarum or York pattern, and the manuscript therefore cannot be assigned to either group. The calendar contains the principal York feasts, but the translations and a number of the minor saints are missing. Additional entries associated with the Order appear, but none seem to have interfered with the York material.

Another interesting example of confusion relates to Bodleian Wood C.12, a Book of Hours whose calendar contains mostly Sarum saints, but includes Wilfrid, John of Beverley, and others associated with York. While van Dijk assigned the manuscript tentatively to Beverley, on the strength of 'two feasts of St John of Beverley in red'[56], the single responsory series in the manuscript (from the office for the Dead) follows the Sarum order, and the manuscript therefore appears in our Sarum group. This illustration seems to support the above evidence that Wilfrid enjoyed veneration outside the use of York; this is not unlikely, given Bede's laudatory account of his life and death.[57]

John's cult, too, was apparently widespread. He was venerated in some areas of the North as early as 80 years after his death and, according to Susan Wilson, the cult was transmitted to the continent 'within a very short period of time'.[58] Victory at Agincourt in 1415, on the day of John's translation, had been attributed to his intercession, and the devotion was promulgated by king Henry and spread throughout Britain. Although unlike William he had never received papal canonization[59], John's feast was observed across the country, at least after Agincourt, and proper material for him added to existing manuscripts including the Launton breviary (Laud misc.299), in which both a calendar entry and proper lessons appear, the sole evidence that, quite against logic, associates this Oxfordshire book with York. The frequency with which John appears, and his ubiquity in the south, may suggest either that he was popular, or that the Henrician initiative to include him in the liturgy of the whole country was successful, depending on the date, as yet ambiguous from the rather late liturgical evidence, when the cult was most successful.

William's cult, however, seems to have been 'a local affair', as Christopher Norton has suggested, which was unsuccessful outside York.[60] His main feastday and Translation are found in every York manuscript without exception, but other than the additions in the Wollaton Antiphonal (a Sarum book whose calendar was evidently modified for use in the northern province) his feasts have so far been located in only a few non-York manuscripts, including the Burnet Psalter now at Aberdeen and possibly linked to Ely, and an Augustinian calendar from Launceston in Cornwall.[61]

It will be clear that the calendar alone should not be a decisive indicator of the liturgical use of a book. Neither should it be considered a reliable summary of the book's contents. Some of the most interesting aspects of the calendar are the changes applied to it — and these are not always followed up with revisions to the contents of the Sanctorale, which would have required an expert hand.

To give one example, a number of feasts, in several hands, were inserted into the calendar of CAdd.2602, including David, Chad, Patrick, Vitalis, and the translations of John of Beverley and Nicholas. Nothing was added to the Sanctorale. If these saints' days were celebrated using the relevant services from the Common of Saints, or if separate libelli were used and are now lost, no indication survives in the present manuscript. It cannot be assumed, as Pfaff writes, that they were celebrated beyond 'some degree of recognition'. Similarly, the calendar of XVI.O.9 contains most of the feasts peculiar to York, but proper material for Germanicus, Batildis, Gilbert, Albinus, Petroc, and Everild does not appear in the Sanctorale. It might be asked whether relevant lessons and texts were available — by the fourteenth century they surely existed.

Other issues in the Sanctorale concern the number of proper lessons provided. This may indicate the extent to which the feast was celebrated (and may indicate its grade, although some feasts with nine lessons at Matins can take up to six from the Common of Saints.) In general, within the York group the number of lessons and prayers for a given feast is quite consistent, although there are a number of exceptions. The Arundel book, on the whole, contains few proper lessons. This may be unsurprising since it is an antiphonal, but, somewhat bewilderingly, it supplies six lessons for Gilbert, perhaps suggesting links to Lincolnshire.

More inconsistent are the proper lessons for the translation of John of Beverley. There are usually three lessons for his main feastday, although the calendar of YAdd.69 specifies nine, and Laud.misc.299, *contains* nine, although these exist as a late addition to the book. On his Translation, however, eight York sources have nine lessons; the remainder have three[62], as do the Sarum sources. The proper lessons for Augustine of Canterbury are also variable: propers of three and nine lessons appear in three manuscripts each.[63] On the whole, though, Sanctorale contents are relatively consistent with their calendars, as long as it is remembered that if a feast is added to the calendar, the likelihood is slim that anything will have been added to the Sanctorale.

The calendar alone, it is clear, is an inadequate indicator of observance, and corroboration must be sought elsewhere. Although it is a much briefer list of saints, the Litany is helpful since it is sometimes not altered along with the calendar (or indeed the other contents of the book). The inclusion of a saint in the original contents of the Litany, which would have been read out loud from beginning to end, should be concrete evidence that a saint's name, at the least, was intended to be invoked in the liturgy.

Similarly the Litany can support other evidence used to assign a book to a use. The calendar of Rawl.C.553, a Book of Hours assigned to our Sarum group, has been altered to include a number of the putative York saints, including Paulinus and Wilfrid, along with the feast of relics. It also shows marks of erasure, Scholastica (11 Feb) being one of the most obvious examples. van Dijk calls it a monastic calendar for St Mary's York 'made into a secular one'. He also writes that the (existing, secular) office of the Dead appears to have been 'corrected for the Use of York'[64]. It is notable that the corrections appear precisely at the points in the responsory series where the York order differs from Sarum. Here, the Litany serves to confirm the suspicion that this manuscript was modified from Sarum order, for it contains few York saints and on the whole follows the Sarum pattern.[65]

A final example demonstrates that different sections of a liturgical manuscript can and should be used to corroborate one another. The calendar of Rawl.G.170, a Psalter, has been heavily modified. Erasures appear on the days appointed for Emerenciana, Babillus, Polycarp, Wilfrid, Aldhelm, Grimbald, Everild, Aidan, Evurtius, Maurillus, the feast of relics, John of Beverley, Germanus, Eustace, and pope Martin. Often the erasures have been done imperfectly, and the name of the saint in question is still somewhat visible. All but Aldhelm are saints found frequently in the York calendar, and seven of them are among the 17 saints found *only* in the York calendar. In their place have been added saints more likely to be found in the Sarum calendar – David,

Richard, Alphege, Frideswide, and others. It would appear that the calendar was originally written for York, and modified for Sarum. This conclusion is supported by the presence of an unmodified York responsory series for the office of the Dead.

The Litany (f. 211v) includes some typical York saints (Paulinus, John, Wilfrid, William, Austreberta, Hilda, and Everild), although Everild's name has been partly erased, and confirms that this part of the book seems to have been originally written for York. As we have seen, modifications to the calendar may not always be reflected in the Litany.

There are also two intriguing marginal notes. At the beginning of the Litany, someone has written 'Ista letania et que sequuntur sunt de usu Eboracensi' — and later, at the beginning of the Dead (f. 220v), the same hand has written as a header 'de usu Eboracensi: non Sarisberiensi'. Although it is unclear whether or not these notes were made at the same time as the alterations to the calendar,[66] it is evident that the contents of the book were surveyed and identified on at least one occasion by someone who was able to tell the difference between the two rites. If the intention was indeed to remove York saints and to replace them with Sarum alternatives, can we suggest, perhaps, that the material erased by the reviser, including saints, was understood to be characteristic of the York rite? If so, we have come much closer to an understanding of what was thought distinctive to the York calendar *at the place and time of the amendments to the manuscript.*

Rawl.G.170 affords an opportunity to discuss briefly a final aspect of the calendar. On several feasts (Paul the hermit, Chad, John of Beverley, Botulph, and Francis) someone has added an equal-armed cross with embellished vertices. The same symbol is used on f. 189r, where a dittographic error (a second instance of Ps 144.6) is crossed through. It might seem as if it denoted a place where the book was to be modified. But a similar symbol is seen in the calendar of YAdd.68 on the feasts of Gilbert, Grimbald, and Wulfranus, and a different cross is added in red to several entries[67] in XVI.O.9. Do these symbols indicate local practices?

What can be concluded about the York calendar and Sanctorale? The distinct properties of the calendars of books already identified as York include entries for various saints (the four allegedly archetypal York saints and others). But the presence of some of these entries is not peculiar to the York books, as witnessed for a few feasts shared with the Sarum group and, more importantly, with manuscripts of varying provenance. Paulinus and Wilfrid, for example, appear in several of Wormald's calendars, and in the post-Conquest calendar Bodleian Add. C. 260 cited by Heslop,[68] and John of Beverley appears in any number of manuscripts. It is, of course, essential to distinguish between their appearance in the original text of the manuscript or as a later addition, a distinction that has not always been made.

Except for Everild and the York Relics, the feasts found only in our York group are not unique to the use, although seventeen of them appear in every York manuscript. Whilst these saints can be added to the list of the common properties of York books, care must be taken not to treat them as indicators of the use. Nor would one be blameless in suggesting that the presence or absence of a feast in a given manuscript means that it was or was not celebrated. The most useful comparative conclusions with respect to the properties of the York calendar will only be possible when the number of non-York calendars under investigation is expanded.

This section has relied upon groups of manuscripts based on common responsory series in order to establish which feasts are characteristic of all York manuscripts, and which are unique to them. It has identified several means whereby the large group of York-series sources can be subdivided, and specific characteristics of a number of books have been identified. The next section will consider analyses of the melodies of sources containing plainsong, another subtle method of comparison that is proximate to textual analysis for a frequently underused component of liturgical manuscripts.

Plainsong

This paper began with the objective to discern some of the distinctive characteristics of the York office. Until now the focus has been on the textual contents of the books, assessing what Cranmer termed 'great diversitie in saying', but to end here would be to ignore evidence that is as much a part of the sources as the responsories, and which conveys just as much information that can be analysed.

The preference here is for abstract comparison of melodies, as one might compare several witnesses of a text, and the objective to supply some observations based on this quantitative method. Not only is it desirable to consider this relatively untouched repertory for its own sake, the collection of melodies provides another set of data from the York manuscripts through which to test, confirm, and question theories based on other aspects of the liturgy explored in preceding sections. Were the text to be absent, erased, or rewritten, identification through surviving fragments of the chants might be helpful.

Predictably little can be found in the Surtees edition relating to plainsong; it is nowhere clear which items may have been set to music. The 1493 printed breviary contains no chant, and no contemporary York rival to the Sarum Antiphonal was ever printed.[69] Few manuscript sources of the York office chants survive; there are four Breviaries (only two of them complete) and a lone Antiphonal. More than twenty years ago, David Hiley and Peter Underwood worked with a number of Mass chants, and Underwood surveyed office chants from the Common of Saints in a single source (Bodleian Gough liturg. 1).[70] No one has yet studied chants of the office Temporale.

The three surviving musical sources of the York Temporale will be compared with several Sarum counterparts through material that is common to both groups; that is, I will compare the plainsong settings of the texts of several Matins responsories for Advent and Holy Week. While observations about the connexion between text and musical setting will arise, the principal objective will be to consider how the music of the York office manuscripts compares with that of Sarum sources and, principally, within the chants of the office liturgy, whether significant melodic variations exist.

The three musical sources of the York Temporale are Arundel, YAdd.69, and Sion. Each contains the characteristic York responsory series for Advent, Holy Week, All Saints, and the Dead. The Sarum sources, drawn from the present Sarum group, also contain the relevant responsory series: these are Laud.misc.299, Wollaton, and CAdd.2602.

As for other aspects of this study, either breadth or depth must be sacrificed, and it is appropriate here to select eight musical items and compare their sources word-by-word. Four responsories and their verses were selected in order to compare melodies where the responsory series differ between the two traditions: Adv.1-MR1 (invariable in its placement in the order of responsories) *Aspiciens a longe* with the verse *quique terrigine*; the text *Ierusalem plantabis* with a variable verse *Deus a Libano* (York) or *Exulta satis* (Sarum), found at Adv2-.MR6 in the York order (Sarum MR5); the text *Suscipe verbum virgo* and the verse *paries quidem,* York's Adv3-MR4 (elsewhere, Adv1-MR5 in Sarum order); and the invariable text for Fri-MR7 *Tradiderunt me* with the verse *astiterunt reges.*

The method for comparison is based solely on the number and pitch of the notes of the melodic setting of a given word, for each of the 171 words in the eight items. All notational variants (those that change the appearance of the music, but do not change the melody) are ignored. These broad forms of analysis produce three significant observations.

The first, concerning the link between the text and its musical setting, is that whenever the text is consistent, so is the music, regardless of the placement of the item within the order of service. The setting, for instance, of *Suscipe verbum virgo* is always basically the same chant, regardless of its differing placement within the responsory series of Sarum and York, for the variants do not change the melody substantially.

Does this relationship seem obvious? It is reasonable that chant should be linked to text, or text to chant, the whole existing consubstantially in the minds of performers of the liturgy. But a second observation contradicts this apparent truth. When the text differs (i.e., where there is a different verse for *Ierusalem plantabis*), the melody for both versions is the same, with slight variants to address the somewhat different lengths of the respective texts. Here, then, the melody is determined not by the text of the verse, but by the responsory or by its musical setting. This is certainly an exception in the chants surveyed, and contradicts the rather consistent picture that seems to indicate that the order of the melodies is dependent upon the order of the texts to which they are invariably set. As for the difference between Sarum and York melodies, it can be said that the music *for any given text common to both* is broadly the same.

The third observation, however, provides slightly greater specificity. While the same basic melody may be present, there are a number of consistent variations between the chants in the York group and their counterparts in the Sarum group. These variations are striking in their uniformity within the manuscripts of each tradition.

Full details of each of the following variants, illustrating the Sarum and York versions of the melodies, appear in Table 5. Several variants occurred in only one manuscript. These have been ignored in the analysis (but noted in the table), as one might ignore a minor textual variant in a single witness, since the comparison of the two repertories will be most effective where they are both internally consistent.

Of the 171 chantwords[71] in the sample, ten have both a Sarum and a York setting that vary in two or more of their pitches. None of these appear obviously to be the result of scribal error (for instance, the accidental transposition of a third through careless copying of pitches to the adjacent line or space on the stave), nor can the variants be characterized in groups. What is significant is that the two traditions have slightly different but internally consistent melodies for these words.

Eleven chantwords varied by a single pitch (comprising one more or one less pitch, depending on perspective). Over half of these occurred in the melody for the Advent 3 text *Suscipe verbum virgo*; the most obvious explanation for extension or shortening of the melody, an alteration in the length of the text, does not appear to be a factor here. Five further chantwords had a repeated pitch added in the same place (i.e. DEF > DDEF). These are perhaps the least significant type of variant, but also the least frequent to occur.

It ought to be underlined that the above variants occur, pitch for pitch, in every manuscript of both traditions, and therefore in 26 out of 171 words, or 15% of the total, two absolutely consistent versions of the melody exist, one for Sarum and the other for York.

Two conclusions arise, which might seem contradictory. First, it is evident that a York 'dialect' exists, accounting for about 15% of the present sample, and that it is coherent. Its consistency (even, or perhaps especially, if it is based on the same apparently trivial variants) leaves little to doubt.[72] This conclusion, though based on limited evidence, seems to confirm the belief, supported by Hiley and Underwood, that Sarum and York sources used rather different chants. It has been hypothesized that York chants, at least for the mass, may have been derived from pre-Conquest material, while Sarum chants were perhaps more Norman.[73]

How did a consistent dialect arise? Did it in fact predate the Norman influence that came to appear in the liturgy of the south? This is a challenging view to support, and compelling evidence has yet to appear. More broadly, what is the significance of a distinct York dialect for common melodies?

The second conclusion, by logic, is that nearly all of the remaining 85% of this York dialect is exactly the same, pitch for pitch, as the prevailing Sarum dialect in these sources, with a few exceptions for single-witness variants. This alternative interpretation of the same result seems to contradict the existing consensus. Even if we should expect the same texts to be set to the same melodies in every case, this uniformity is notable.

Lisa Colton has suggested, on the basis of other evidence, that it is not unthinkable that later York polyphony (the York Masses) might have been based on characteristically Sarum chants.[74] The present observations obscure the distinction between the two and make this proposition even less unthinkable. We should certainly not disbelieve that chants *apparently* associated with Sarum were known, and used, in York. The existence of several manuscripts with Sarum contents, including music, that were adapted for use in the province of York (Wollaton, for example) also confirms this proposal.

The identical material (closer to 80% if we exclude both the consistent variants and those in a single manuscript) does suggest either that one tradition is derived from the other, which seems dubious, or that Sarum and York have some common origin, a possibility which will be discussed in the next section of this study. Certainly the appearance of chants in one tradition should not now preclude the possibility of their appearance in the other. Since the present melodic settings of responsories appear consistently in the Sarum group, it could be said that they are characteristic of the Sarum tradition. But they also appear, just as consistently, in the York books. Perhaps they appear there in their own right, and not because one tradition should be linked to the other, at least in a derivative way.

The present results inspire an extension of the analysis, for it appears that the musical material employed in the York tradition, a pattern of liturgy of a church which always emphasized its independence from Southern hegemony, differs much less than might be expected from Sarum chants. But it ought to be highlighted that to a significant degree York liturgy did incorporate some unique melodic material to accompany its unique, consistent patterns of text. In this section, a third aspect of the York office liturgy has been elucidated, and a similar result obtained: as for preceding comparisons, some material is present that is quite consistent within the books identified as for York, but it is accompanied by patterns that are not absolutely restricted to them.

Summary

From the contents of several lists of potential sources of the York office, a large group of manuscripts was identified whose responsory series matched the established York pattern as defined by existing scholarship. A smaller group, possessing certain characteristics apparently related to York, was also determined to have responsory series consistent with the Sarum pattern. The reasons for the previous association of these manuscripts with York were outlined. Having identified with certainty the York group, we then pursued an examination of some of their obvious characteristics to determine the properties common to each of the sources, and some of the inconsistencies between them.

It has been possible to identify two potential groups of manuscripts based on these analyses: first, the Sion and Cosin books share four uncommon saints in their calendars. More convincingly, the manuscripts YAdd.69 and 70 along with Laud.misc.84 share a total of 16 lessons unique to them; and their calendars also demonstrate similarity. These three sources do not appear otherwise to be related, but further study is certainly warranted.

While the responsories and verses of the York group may have been consistent, evidence from their Matins lessons, calendars, and from the Sanctorale demonstrates that the manuscripts are prone to significant variation. About 15% of the plainchant in York books is distinct from the complementary Sarum chants, but much more is shared between the two traditions — more, perhaps, than the other types of variation, or the reputed independence of the two provinces in all things, might suggest. Numerous types of evidence — order of texts, lessons, lists of saints, proper material, music — appear to support a principal conclusion. The responsory series should be seen as the most reliable single method of comparison. There are other properties characteristic to all York books, but few are exclusive to them, at least among those which are easily identifiable. Assignment to a liturgical use, then, ought not to be based on a single aspect of a manuscript.

The York liturgy in context

Liturgical analysis has established that each complete office manuscript whose assignment to York is reasonably certain provides particular Matins responsory series identified as characteristic of the use. The Advent series is identical to the normative Advent series for York in *CAO*; others have been identified for the Triduum, All Saints, and the office of the Dead. No other common feature of the manuscripts associated with York seems to be as consistent as this distinctive set of responsory series. In light of this fact, and given the considerable diversity of series recorded in *CAO*, it is worth noting that the patterns of the York responsory series show some similarities with certain series from Normandy. This potential relation suggests that the post-Conquest liturgy in York may reflect a tendency of imported Norman clerics to favour patterns of liturgy that would have been familiar to them.

Dondi shows that, at least for the sources of All Saints known to Beyssac and Gy, the series from Sées is identical to the York series. The same pattern appears in the All Saints series of the Holy Sepulchre liturgy, another rite with a potentially Norman origin.[75] *CAO* supplies similar hints for Advent: Hesbert's series for Bayeux and the common series collected from the York manuscripts are identical on both the first and third Sundays of Advent except for the last responsory of each service, although the common pattern of the preceding responsories can be found in the series from various cathedrals. It should be noted that the York series collected for Advent 1 is identical to that of Mâcon and differs by one responsory from that of Rouen; the series for Advent 4 is identical with a single exception from that of Cambrai; and the order for quarter days in Advent in the York sources is identical to that of Saint-Vaast and of Mont-Saint-Eloi.[76] In the office for the Dead, Ottosen notes that four responsories used for the recitation of the York office on All Souls' Day are found together elsewhere only in two sources from Caen and Rouen, and the York responsory series differs by only one text from that of Rouen.[77] Although Dondi writes that the Holy Sepulchre and York books appear to be related by a common antecedent,[78] no indisputable connexion to Bayeux, or to another single Norman tradition, seems absolutely clear in any of the responsory series I have collected. Nevertheless the several series held in common by York and Normandy sources should be noted carefully.[79]

Connexions between post-Conquest English rites and Norman liturgy have already been proposed. Based on evidence from the texts, Edmund Bishop suggested that the use of Rouen was a natural and potential source of Norman-inspired English liturgy after the Conquest; he goes to some length to link the liturgies of Holy Week found in sources of Rouen and of Hereford. He was less confident of the reputed relation between Rouen and Sarum, for the common features were 'items which, practically speaking... formed part of the substructure of all the late medieval uses'.[80] Hill and Brooke, however, suggest that Rouen was likely the source of Sarum customs up to 1100; this tradition would have been an influence on the 'new pattern' of ritual that was emerging in both provinces in the last decade of the eleventh century.[81] A shared Norman ancestor to both Sarum and York, then, does not seem out of the question.

Surviving records certainly suggest that bishops across England oversaw liturgical matters within their jurisdiction, and had the capacity both to assess and identify liturgical books and to attempt to enforce standards. The prevalence of episcopal legislation concerning 'use' and liturgy suggests that it was a subject of some concern.

Among the most frequent references are orders that certain saints' days should be celebrated. The Sarum Constitutions of Richard Poore (ca. 1221) prescribe the observance of Thomas Becket's Translation (7 July) and the deposition of Wulfstan (19 January); Poore is also reportedly the first, in 1223, to use the iconic phrase 'secundum usum Sarum'.[82] An interesting set of prescriptions is found in the three groups of statutes for Winchester: first the feasts for Swithun and Birinus, patrons of the bishopric, are added, and then the feasts of other saints whose remains were in the diocese were to be added to the calendar and to be celebrated.[83] Walter de Cantilupe, bishop of Worcester, ordered before 1250 that saints Dominic and Francis should have nine lessons.[84] John Grandisson of Exeter (bishop 1327–69) also appeared to exert some control over the veneration of local saints.[85] Archiepiscopal sanction continued into the fifteenth century: Roger Walden ordered in 1398 that the feasts of David (1 March) and Chad (2 March) along with Winifred (3 Nov) should be observed, and Henry Chichele gave these three feasts along with that of St George the dignity of nine lessons.[86]

Other records indicate an interest in the use observed rather than specific feasts. This may suggest that ordinary rather than proper texts were also under scrutiny. Certainly the canon of the mass seems to have been important: a statute for peculiars of Durham in the diocese of York (1241 x 1249) refers to the York canon.[87] Deficiencies were also observed: in a 1300 visitation the Dean of Salisbury discovered a gradual 'non de usu' at Roscomp, and recorded the presence of a manual at Sandhurst, 'sed non est de usu Sarum'.[88] The visitation records of Grandisson's predecessors note several books 'non de usu ex toto', and another 'totaliter insufficiens'.[89] As for the North, a 1323 communication from Archbishop William Melton of York urges the Augustinian priory of Hexham to adopt 'usum ecclesie nostre Ebor'.[90]

Concern about the provision of specific liturgical uses can also be found in the statutes of several cathedral foundations. It is certainly possible to suggest that these references might pertain to broadly non-liturgical matters, for instance the diverse contents of a Customary or Ordinal, not all of which deal with the liturgy. Much of the first volume of Frere's *The Use of Sarum* concerns itself with such documentation.[91] But the examples below, a representative sample, refer specifically to the canon of the Mass and the provision of service books.

The language used in some of the legislation is quite similar. Powicke and Cheney suggest that the Canterbury statutes (1213 x 1214) form the model adopted by other diocesan authorities: Salisbury's statutes (1217 x 1219) bear a considerable resemblance to them, and in Chichester (1245 x 1252) the word-order is slightly different, but the vocabulary and intention seem identical.[92] The passages illustrate a concern that the texts (as represented by the canon of the mass and by service books) should be consistent with some model use, although the specific properties of this model are never outlined.

Another series of episcopal prescriptions is more confusing. We have pointed to elements where the liturgical evidence from Sarum and York appears to correspond. Late thirteenth-century letters of Antony Bek, bishop of Durham, which enjoined the colleges of Chester-le-Street (1286) and St Andrew, Bishops Auckland (1292) to adopt the 'modum psallendi secundum usum Eborum vel Salesberie' may suggest that the differences were not very significant or that either was acceptable. Surprisingly the order is repeated in 1428 by the then bishop Thomas Longley.[93] The innocuous 'vel' seems to question the premise that these two major, well-defined liturgies, competing for primacy, were very different from one another. A similar option exists in copies of the c.1258 statutes of Wells, in which the canon of the mass 'quod est in ecclesia Eboracensi vel Saresbiriensi correctus' was to be used.[94] An order of archbishop Godfrey of Ludham for York in 1259, however, refers to books 'secundum usum ecclesie nostre Ebor vel saltem Sar', which apparently expresses a preference.[95]

A 1293 statute of York supplies a list of all the *festa duplicia* to be observed in the province. Comparing this document with the collected calendars of the York group manuscripts, it seems that each feast in the list does appear and is listed as a double in all sources that supply the class of the feast.[96] Whilst the sources are considerably more recent than the statute, the promulgation of the feasts in question was evidently successful. The inconsistency on other occasions in the calendar suggests that the consistency does not exist by chance. In the same document, a special prescription declares William's translation on 8 January to be a double feast; in most manuscripts his feast is marked with a rubric indicating the feast is a *duplum festum principale*, and a note that it should be celebrated on the first Sunday following Epiphany.

It has been suggested that Norman authorities did exert an influence on the existing liturgical practices they encountered. Such policies are most frequently associated with Lanfranc, the first Norman archbishop of Canterbury, who has been credited generally with a 'purge' of the Anglo-Saxon calendar that supposedly removed a number of saints, among them those for whom reliable documentation could not be found.[97] From the council at Winchester in 1072 onward, Lanfranc's interest in revision seems to have been ongoing.[98] In a comparison of pre- and post-Conquest calendars associated with Christ Church, Canterbury Heslop noted 27 saints had disappeared in the latter, some 'of Anglo-Saxon national importance'.[99]

Jay Rubenstein has provoked doubts concerning the motive for the revision. While Lanfranc may have been responsible for 'relatively minor calendrical housekeeping', Rubenstein attributes any malevolent motive for the omission of Anglo-Saxon saints to the interpretation of Christ Church historian Eadmer who may have thought it a deliberate attack on existing practices.[100] Richard Pfaff believes that there was no uniform Anglo-Saxon calendar from which it would be possible to prove that a set of inferior saints was removed, and that the pre-Conquest liturgy, like its late medieval successor, was characterised by local practices and regional variation; moreover, the apparent revival in the thirteenth century of the observance of Anglo-Saxon saints, some 'of considerable obscurity',[101] explains away the otherwise provocative appearance of minor saints with Anglo-Saxon names in late medieval calendars. But these arguments suggest only that the purported introduction of Norman practices may not have been an ideological or deliberately didactic act, and that it is difficult to know what came before. Certainly any Norman influence on the liturgy of York does not seem to have been destructive to local Anglo-Saxon saints, some of whom appear among the seventeen characteristic York feasts.

Returning to the question of Norman influence on broader liturgical patterns, it would be most helpful to identify individual figures who might have been responsible for the imposition of foreign liturgy. But the possibilities are numerous and are difficult to distinguish, for a great many of king William's appointees to various posts in the English liturgical establishment were closely linked to the court and the secular cathedrals of Normandy.[102] For Hereford, Bishop suggested, we can assume that the cleric in question was in place before the loss of Normandy which, while an obvious conclusion, 'is all that can be asserted with anything like confidence'. He proposes Robert de Bethune, bishop of Hereford from 1131 to 1148, who is said to have 'renewed the celebration of the divine offices'.[103] There is also a manuscript (British Library Royal 8 D.vii) of the twelfth century, copied at Llanthony, which contained Rouen ceremonial, putting it in contact with Bethune.[104] Based on a relation between the liturgical patterns of Hereford and Rouen with those of York, Dondi notes that the vector between them may have been Gerard, formerly precentor at Rouen and later bishop of Hereford (1096–1100) and archbishop of York (1100–1108).[105]

At York itself, however, one individual seems a more likely candidate. Lanfranc's northern counterpart and William's appointee to the see of York was Thomas of Bayeux, once a clerk of Odo of Bayeux who had studied in Laon as well as in Germany and Spain.[106] According to the chronicle of Hugh the Chanter, he was 'a distinguished and very learned clerk ... renowned throughout the provinces of Gaul and well beyond for his learning, honour, and distinction'.[107] Thomas was archbishop for close to thirty years and, as Hugh notes, was responsible for rebuilding the church in York: '[He] found everything laid waste as a result of enemy action ...' More to the point, 'he founded and built the present church, and adorned and furnished it to the best of his power with clerks, *books*, and ornaments'.[108] On this point Hugh confirms what must have been the case; the books, along with the Anglo-Saxon Minster, had been destroyed by fire[109]; new liturgical manuscripts would certainly have been needed in order to carry out the services. Returning to the assumption that newly-founded establishments would have liturgies based on those which were authoritative in the minds of the founders, we ought first to turn to Bayeux.

Given that the books of the Anglo-Saxon Minster were destroyed, new models would have been sought, and the predictable exemplar would certainly have been a rite with which the new arrivals were familiar. But the absolute evidence for such hypotheses remains elusive.

Conclusions

Ninety years ago, Edmund Bishop wrote that the comparison of liturgical books 'is an enquiry most tedious ... [and] only by an accumulation of evidence in detail [can] a fair and reasonable presumption ... be raised'.[110] His observation remains true. The very hallmark of empirical liturgical research, its seemingly endless comparison of similar sources, is both the property that causes most scholars to avoid it and the most efficient method to determine the characteristics of the liturgy of a given region. This study has examined most of the surviving manuscripts of the York office, and it is now possible, for the first time, to speak with some confidence about their distinctive characteristics.

The York set of responsory series is identified as the most prominent characteristic unique to the manuscripts of York use. It also seems likely that this was already understood in the fifteenth century, for the sole series in Rawl.C.553, a Sarum book modified for York, has been altered to suit the York order, and marginal notes in Rawl.G.170 identify its office for the Dead as that of York. Links between the York liturgy and its potential Norman antecedents by means of responsory series may exist, suggesting that new orders of service may have been brought to England by Norman authorities, but the similarities are not conclusive enough for the link to be absolutely certain. The limited extent of the present enquiry demands expansion.

Like the responsory series, the York plainchant is also distinct; 15% of all words surveyed have a musical setting that is both consistent and different from the corresponding Sarum melody. Other aspects of the York books, while they may be common to many of the sources, are more varied: it has been shown that the four putative 'York saints', until now a frequent means of assignment, are among a list of saints whose feastdays are often characteristic of but not exclusive to York manuscripts. The only feasts absolutely unique to York are those of Everild and of the York relics. This is not to suggest that the seventeen feasts peculiar to the York group manuscripts are not distinctive constituents of the use: they are, and the modification of manuscripts (Wollaton, for example) to include or exclude them seems to indicate their significance. But some of these feasts, especially those of John of Beverley and of the foreign or non-Northern saints, were observed outside York's sphere of influence, and their usefulness as *indicators* of the use is therefore to be questioned.

It appears that material associated with Sarum was not unknown in the northern province: the Wollaton Antiphonal was certainly used in the eponymous parish, although almost all of its contents, including antiphons, responsories, and lessons, were written for Sarum.[111] That some 80% of the York music studied is identical to comparable Sarum melodies seems to suggest a considerable degree of similarity between the two traditions. While this last finding may be meaningless in a wider context where other English or French uses may well have employed the same chants, it is notable in the present enquiry, an examination of a regional English use in relation to the dominant use that surrounded it, that the two appear to have used much of the same plainchant repertory. Likewise, the fact that several episcopal directions required churches to adopt either Sarum or York use seems to suggest less functional difference between the two than might be expected. If both had their roots in rites imported around the same time by the Normans, the ambivalence about which use to adopt may be provocative.

Explanations for these observations, especially keeping in mind the earlier conclusions which highlight York's distinctiveness, demand answers to challenging questions: why was any particular form of liturgy adopted or preferred? Presumably texts were not reordered or modified without reason. While the observance of saints' days may vary understandably from place to place, why would one particular order of the common texts (i.e. the responsory series) be favoured? Surely because it was customary. Conclusions about this matter may suggest why certain forms of liturgy were adopted or modified by the Norman authorities. Succeeding stages of this project will examine issues of variation through continued study of the texts and their descent.

There are several implications arising from this preliminary enquiry that ought to be outlined. First, the several books that contain both York saints and Sarum responsory series should be removed from the lists of York manuscripts. The Antiphonal at Arundel Castle is therefore the sole surviving manuscript of its genre from York, and the description of its contents should be expedited.[112] Among the Sarum group, the importance of the Wollaton Antiphonal should be emphasized[113] and its modifications for York use studied in full, since they may illustrate what were understood to be the key differences between the two uses. It would also be interesting to explore the implications of the printed breviary on the stability of the use: while the calendar and lessons of the 1493 breviary may not have been representative of the manuscript tradition, the increasing number of printed copies may have had a normalizing effect on what was understood by the use of York, at least by the time of Cranmer's preface.[114]

It ought to be pointed out that the manuscripts themselves are not uniform. The term 'use' may itself imply a greater uniformity than ever existed; the fact that it has been used as a standard descriptor has undoubtedly contributed to the view that the liturgical pattern of any given use did not change from book to book. If there is any lesson to be learned, it is that *usus Eboracensis* obviously meant something to its contemporaries — *although what it meant undoubtedly varied from time to time and from place to place*. The context, therefore, needs to be determined in every case. Preoccupation with a single genre of evidence is to be discouraged; as has been seen above, observations based on one aspect can often be corroborated with evidence from another.

With this mandate in mind, it is now necessary to examine at a greater level of detail the variations and relations among the manuscripts. All of the York sources are related, but they are also variable in significant and interesting ways. The next stage of this project will involve the editing of a number of offices from the manuscripts of the York Sanctorale, and, where present, from the other insular liturgical traditions. The identification and grouping of variants would help to describe the descent of the York office, and, indeed, may identify the exemplars used for the first printed breviary of 1493, but it would also support anticipated work on the relations between the several minor regional uses and the dominant Sarum use, and discernible interactions between them. Given the omnipresence of the liturgy in the context of numerous disciplines, this ongoing project ought to be a useful contribution to the study of the medieval church in northern England.

Thu	CAdd 3110	XVI .O.9	YAdd 383	YAdd 115	YAdd 69	YAdd 70	YAdd 68	Laud. misc.84	Sion	1493
MR1	qss	qss	qss	qss	qss	qss	qss	qss	qss	qss*
MR2	ppi	vsl	mip	vsl	vsl	vsl	ppi	vsl	mip	mip
MR3	mip	rei	fsh	eee-2	rei	rei	mip	rej	fsh	fsh
MR4	edo	edo	eom	edo	ede	edo	edo	edo	edo	edo*
MR5	een	dee	een	ees	iee	iee	dee	iee	een	een
MR6	qei	qoi	eee-1	atc	eho	eho	een	eho	eho	eho
MR7	fcv	fcv	fcv	fcv	fcv	fcv	fcv	fcv	fcn	fcn
MR8	ndn	ndn	ndn	ndv	eea	eea	ndn	eea	eea	eea
MR9	eea	eea	eea	eea	iqm-2	iqm-2	eea	iqm-2	qoe	sec

Fri	CAdd 3110	XVI .O.9	YAdd 383	YAdd 115	YAdd 69	YAdd 70	YAdd 68	Laud. misc.84	Sion	1493
MR1	qoc	msm	qoc	qoc	qoc	qoc	msm	qoc	qoc	qoc*
MR2	cii	dem	cii	cii	tas	tas	ope	tas	tas	cii
MR3	tas	ice	fed	fed	rda	qoq	qoq	rda	rda	fed
MR4	etg	eug	etg	eug	eug	eug	etg	etg	etg	etg*
MR5	pes	ncd	qsm	ned	qdi	qdi	ncd	qdi	ned	sql
MR6	tae	qfp	ies	neq	rse	rse	qfp	rse	neq	qdi
MR7	ffi	ffi	ffi	ffi	ffi	ffi	ffi	ffi	ffi	ffi*
MR8	cqe	cqe	cqe	hep	hep	hep	cqe	neh	hep	oan
MR9	hep	hep	neh	onp	onp	onp	hep	sec	onp	onq

Sat	CAdd 3110	XVI .O.9	YAdd 383	YAdd 115	YAdd 69	YAdd 70	YAdd 68	Laud. misc.84	Sion	1493
MR1	qoc	qoc	**qoe**	**qoe**	**qoe**	**qoe**	cct	**qoe**	**qoe**	**qoe***
MR2	sel	esi	sel	sel	**all**	**all**	pdt	qvv	sel	**all**
MR3	qvv	otd	qvv	eme	des	die	fdq	mmm	eme	*cne*
MR4	**aha**	and	**aha**	**aha**	**aha**	**aha**	vsq-2	**aha**	**aha**	**aha***
MR5	iic	def	aha	aha	**aeh**	**aeh**	nio	ind	aha	**aeh**
MR6	ahe	iqm-1	aeh	uef	ahe	ahe	hem	aha	uef	*ied*
MR7	vas	vas	vas	**vsq-1**	vas	vas	vas	**vsq-1**	vas	**vsq-1**
MR8	ieh	ieh	fhp	ieh	qas	qas	qas	**qai**	iee	**qai**
MR9	qai	qai	-	esq	**sns**	**sns**	cat	**sns**	esq	**sns**

Table 3 - Lessons for Matins during the Triduum from the nine manuscripts containing lessons for these days; the column at far right indicates the lessons in the 1493 edition.

The following pages expand all abbreviations in the preceding table. Texts appearing in bold type appear in the 1493 edition; those in italics appear in the edition only; those marked with an asterisk are used for a lesson both in the edition and the majority of the manuscripts. Texts in roman type (the majority) appear only in the manuscripts.

aeh	**accessit ergo homo (ad cor altum)**	**fed**	**factus est dominus**
aha*	**accedet homo ad (cor altum)**	**ffi**	**fratres festinemus ingredi**
ahe	accedet homo et (quod deus)	fhp	factus hanc pro
all	**adhesit lingua lactantis**	**fsh**	**facti sunt hostes**
and	ammonet nos dilectissum	hem	huius ergo mortem
atc	alii timentes consentiebant	hep	habentes ergo pontificem
cat	cum autem trahit	ice	id circo ergo
cct	cui comparabo te	*ied*	*ipse enim dixit*
cii	**confregit in ira**	iee	inde est et
cne	*candidiores nazarei eius*	ieh	iuste etiam hanc
cqe	compagnum quoque et	ies	ipse enim sciebat
dee	dicamus ergo et	iic	in ipsa civitate
def	dicit enim fratres	ind	ipse non dixit
dem	de excelso misit	iqm-1	in quod malum
des	denigrata est super	iqm-2	itaque quicumque mandu-
die	de ingrata est		caverint
ede	exaudi deus eripe (me)	**mip**	**migravit iuda propter**
edo*	**exaudi deus orationem**	mmm	manus mulierum miseri-
eea	**ego enim accepi**		cordium
eee-1	exaudiebantur ergo et	msm	manum suam misit
eee-2	et egressus est	ncd	nam cum dixisset
een	**ergo exaudivi non**	ndn	numquam domos non
ees	ergo exaudivi sunt	ned	numque et dominum
eho	**ergo hoc orat**	neh	non enim evimus
eme	et maior effecta	neq	nostis ei quibus
eom	exaudi orationem meam	nio	nam ipsum o[illeg.]
esi	et succendit in	*oan*	*omnia autem nuda*
esq	et sabbato quidem	onp	omnis namque pontifex
etg*	**exacuerunt tanquam gladium**	ope	omneis populis eius
eug	exacuerunt ut gladium	otd	oblivioni tradidit dominus
fcv	fratres convenientibus vobis[1]	pes	primus enim sagitta
fcn	**fratres convenientibus nobis**	pdt	propheti dixerunt tibi
fdq	fecit dominus quid	ppi	plorans ploravit in
		qai	**quod autem in**

qas	quod autem sancte
qdi	**quod dicit intenderit**
qei	quis ei invocavit
qfp	quid fecit pilatus
qoc*	**quomodo obtexit caligine**
qoe*	**quomodo obscuratum est**
qoi	quid orabat ista
qoq	quos omnes qui
qsm	qui sagittam mittit
qss*	**quomodo sedet sola**
qvv	qui vescebantur voluptuose
rda	repulit dominus altare
rei	recordata est ierusalem
rse	repente sagittabunt eum
sec	**similiter et calicem**
sel	sed et lamie
sns	**sepulto namque sexta**
sql	*sed quem laterent*
tae	tamen audiamus eos
tas	tetendit arcum suum
vas	vespere autem sabbati
uef	unde ex formum
vas	vespere autem sabbati
vsl	viae syon lugent
vsq-1	**vespere sabbati que**
vsq-2	visi sunt quidem

[1] This is the reading in all but one source and the edition (both of which read nobis); and stems from 1 Cor 11.20.

Table 4 – Differences between the calendars of the York and Sarum groups

Date	York series	Sarum series
5 Jan	No Oct. Thomas Becket **Dep. Edward confessor** in 9 mss (see 7 Jan)	**Oct. Thomas Becket**
Sun. post	**Transl. William**, except for YAdd68, YAdd.70, Cosin, Laud.misc.84, BLAdd.30511	nothing
7 Jan	**Dep Edward confessor** in YAdd.68, Add.70, and Cosin	nothing
8 Jan	**Transl. William** in YAdd.68, YAdd.70, Cosin, Laud.misc.84, BLAdd.30511	**Lucian**
10 Jan	**Paul hermit**	nothing
13 Jan	**Hilary and Remigius** (Hilary only in YAdd.68, Laud.misc.84)	**Hilary only**
17 Jan	**Antony**	**Sulpicius**
18 Jan	**Prisca**; not in Gough.lit.1; not in Sanctorale of XVI.O.9	**Prisca**
19 Jan	**Germanicus**; replaces Wulfstan except in XVI.O.9/O.23; not in Sanctorale of XVI.O.9; not in Gough.lit.1	**Wulfstan**
23 Jan	**Emerentiana**; not in XVI.O.23; takes Common in XVI.O.9 and Arundel	nothing
24 Jan	**Babillus**; not in XVI.O.23; takes Common in XVI.O.9 and Arundel	nothing
25 Jan	**Conv. St Paul**; with St Praejectus in XVI.O.9, YAdd.69, Cosin, Arundel, Laud.misc.84	**Conv. St Paul**
26 Jan	**Polycarp**; takes Common in Arundel	nothing
28 Jan	**Oct. Agnes**; 9 lessons in YAdd68	**Oct. Agnes**
30 Jan	**Batildis**; not in Sanctorale of XVI.O.9	**Batildis**
3 Feb	**Blaise**; added to Rawl C.533	**Blaise**
4 Feb	**Gilbert**; added to Rawl C.533; not in Sanctorale of XVI.O.9; 9 lessons in Arundel	nothing
11 Feb	**Scholastica** only in Rawl C.553, erased.	nothing
24 Feb	**Matthias**; takes Common in Cosin	**Matthias**
1 Mar	**Albinus**; not in Sanctorale of XVI.O.9	**David**; added to CAdd.2602, but not to its Sanctorale
2 Mar	**Chad** added only to Sion, Add 383, Cosin; present in original contents of YAdd 69	**Chad**; not in Sanctorale of CAdd.2602

7 Mar	**Perpetua / Felicitas** generally absent; possibly erased from YAdd.115; in Calendar but not Sanctorale of Cosin	**Perpetua / Felicitas**
8 Mar	nothing	**Felix bishop** of Dunwich added to Harley.2785, Laud.misc.299
12 Mar	**Gregory;** not in Calendar of YAdd.115	**Gregory**
17 Mar	**Patrick** generally absent, but added to Calendar of YAdd.69, but not to its Sanctorale	**Patrick** added to Calendar of CAdd.2602, not to its Sanctorale
20 Mar	**Cuthbert;** defaced in Sanctorale of YAdd.69	**Cuthbert**
21 Mar	**Benedict;** defaced in Sanctorale of YAdd.69; cut out of Gough.lit.1	**Benedict**
2 Apr	**Visitatio BVM** generally absent; but added to Sion, Cosin (not in either Sanctorale); with explanatory note 'pro mandatum sinodale'	nothing
3 Apr	nothing	**Richard** (of Chichester) in Harley.2785, Laud. misc.299
4 Apr	**Ambrose;** 3 lessons in Laud.misc.84	**Ambrose**
14 Apr	**Tyburtius/Valerian;** 9 lessons in XVI.O.23 (usu 3)	**Tyburtius/Valerian**
24 Apr	**Wilfrid** generally present with 3 lc; Arundel gives 'ut in festo sancti Ambrosii'; defaced in YAdd.69, 70.	nothing
27 Apr	**Sytha** in Sion, XVI.O.23, and Cosin (never in Sanctorale)	nothing
28 Apr	**Vitalis;** prayer only in YAdd.68, Arundel; absent in CAdd.3110	**Vitalis;** not in Sanctorale of CAdd.2602
29 Apr	nothing	**Transl. Edmund** king and martyr in Harley.2785 **Dep. Erkenwald** in CAdd.2602
1 May	**Philip and James;** missing in YAdd.383; added to Calendar of YAdd.115	**Philip and James**
3 May	**Inv. Holy Cross, Alexander, Eventius;** also **Theodore** in Laud.misc.84, YAdd.69 and 115; added to Sion	**Inv. Holy Cross, Alexander, Eventius**

7 May	**John of Beverley** generally present; defaced in YAdd.69; Arundel gives only prayer and 'ut sup de s ambrosio'	**John of Beverley** added to CAdd.2602, Laud.misc.299 (not in Sanctorale of 2602; but in added leaves of Laud)
9 May	nothing	**Transl. Nicholas** added to all; (not in Sanctorale of CAdd.2602; in new leaves of Laud)
10 May	**Gordian/Epimachus**; oratio only in YAdd.69, Arundel; likewise Nereus (12 May); Urban (25 May); Boniface (5 June); Mark/Marcellian (18 June); Gervase and Protase (19 June)	**Gordian/Epimachus**
25 May	**Urban**	**Aldhelm**
26 May	**Augustine of Canterbury**; (with **Bede** in Sion, YAdd 68, 69, 70; Cosin; Laud.misc.84.) Varying lessons: 3 in Gough.lit.1, Arundel, XVI.O.9; 9 in YAdd 115; BLAdd.30511 and 38624. The rest, 6 lessons.	**Augustine of Canterbury**; (mistakenly labelled *epi et doct* in CAdd.2602)
4 Jun	**Petroc**, generally present; not in Sanctorale of XVI.O.9	nothing
8 Jun	**William of York**	**Medard/Gildard**
11 Jun	**Barnabas**; 3 lessons in XVI.O.9; 9 lessons in YAdd 68, BLAdd.30511	**Barnabas**
12 Jun	**Basilides/Curinus**: not in YAdd.68; also Nazarii in CAdd.3110, Laud.misc.84	**Basilides/Curinus**
15 Jun	**Vitus et al** (Sion, YAdd.383); or **Oct. William**, the rest; often WITH Vitus et al (XVI.O.23, YAdd.68, 69, 115, Cosin, CAdd.3110, BLAdd.30511, 38624, Laud. misc.84, Gough.lit.1	**Vitus et al**
16 Jun	**Ciricus & Julitta**	**Transl. Richard** added to CAdd.2602; **Ciricus & Julitta**
17 Jun	**Botulph**; all but CAdd.3110	nothing
21 Jun	**Leufrid**	nothing
22 Jun	**Alban**; 6 or 9 lessons	**Alban**
26 Jun	**John and Paul**; 9 lessons in YAdd.68	**John and Paul**
28 Jun	**Leo**; not in Sanctorale of XVI.O.23	**Leo**

2 Jul	**Swithun**	**Swithun** added to YAdd.2602, Harley 2785; **Visit BVM** added to Laud. misc.299
6 Jul	**Oct. Peter & Paul**; not in CAdd.3110	**Oct. Peter & Paul** in Harley 2785, Laud. misc.299
8 Jul	**Grimbald**	**Relics** (Sarum) in CAdd.2602, Harley 2785
9 Jul	**Everild**; not in Sanctorale of XVI.O.9	nothing
16 Jul	nothing	**Transl. Osmund** in CAdd.2602; not Harley 2785; added to Laud.misc.299
22 Jul	**Mary Magdalene** (and **Wandrille** in Sion, YAdd.69, 115, 383; Cosin; BLAdd.30511; Laud.misc.84; Gough.lit.1)	**Mary Magdalene** (and **Wandrille** in all)
25 Jul	**James** (and Christopher in Sion, YAdd.69, 383; CAdd 3110; Cosin, Laud.misc.84)	**James** (and Christopher in CAdd.2602, Harley 2785)
27 Jul	**Martha**	**7 Brothers**
28 Jul	**Sampson and Pantaleon** in all but Rawl.C.553, XVI.O.9, YAdd 68, 70; BLAdd.38624	**Sampson** (and **Pantaleon**, Laud. misc.299)
5 Aug	**Oswald**	**Dominic** (labelled *non Sar sed synodalis* in Laud.misc.299)
6 Aug	**Sixtus et al**; (XVI.O.23: labelled *non transfig. dni*)	**Sixtus et al** (Laud. misc.299 has Transfiguration in margin)
7 Aug	**Donatus** (Holy Name added to Cosin, YAdd.69)	**Donatus** (Laud. misc.299 has Holy Name in margin)
8 Aug	**Oct. Peter**	**Oct. Peter, Ciriacus**
17 Aug	**Oct. Lawrence** all but BLAdd.38624	**Oct. Lawrence** in Harley 2785, Laud. misc.299
18 Aug	**Agapitus**; all but BLAdd.38624	**Agapitus**
19 Aug	**Magnus**; all but BLAdd.38624	**Magnus**

23 Aug	nothing	**Timothy et al**
25 Aug	**Hilda**; (not in Sion or Arundel)	nothing
28 Aug	**Augustine (of Hippo)** (and **Hermes** in Sion, YAdd 69, Cosin, Arundel, CAdd.3110, BLAdd.30511, Laud.misc.84, Gough.lit.1)	**Augustine** (and **Hermes** in Laud. misc.299)
31 Aug	**Aidan**	**Cuthberga**
1 Sep	**Giles**	**Giles** (and **Priscus** in Harley 2785, Laud. misc.299)
3 Sep	nothing	**Ordinatio St Gregory** in CAdd.2602 (but not in Sanctorale)
7 Sep	**Evurtius**; all except Arundel, BLAdd.38624	nothing
13 Sep	**Maurillus** all except YAdd.69, Arundel, BLAdd.38624, Gough.lit.1	nothing
15 Sep	**Oct. Nat. BVM** except BLAdd.38624	**Oct. Nat. BVM**; memorial of Nicomedes
16 Sep	**Eufemia et al**	**Edith**
1 Oct	**Remigius et al**	**Remigius**, memorial of **Meliorus** in Harley 2785, Laud. misc.299)
2 Oct	**Thomas of Hereford** (and **Leodegar** in all but Sion, XVI.O.23, YAdd.68, 70, 115)	**Leodegar** in CAdd.2602; **Thomas of Hereford** and Leod. in Harley 2785; Thomas first, with Leod. added, in Laud.misc.299.
4 Oct	**Francis**; all but Sion	**Francis** added to Harley 2785, Laud. misc.299
8 Oct	**Pelagia**; all but Sion	nothing
10 Oct	**Paulinus**	**Gereon**
12 Oct	**Wilfrid**	nothing
16 Oct	nothing	**Michael** *in monte tumba*
17 Oct	nothing	**Etheldreda** added to Laud.misc.299; also added to Sanctorale

18 Oct	**Luke;** and **Justus** (of Beauvais) in Sion, Rawl.C.553, YAdd 68, 69, 70	**Luke**
19 Oct	**Relics (York)**	**Frideswide** added to Laud.misc.299 (not in Sanctorale)
20 Oct	**Austreberta**; all, but not in Sanctorale of YAdd 69	nothing
25 Oct	**Transl. John of Beverley** all, but added to Rawl.C.553	**Crispin and Crispinian; Transl. John of Beverley** added to Harley 2785, Laud.misc.299
30 Oct	**Germanus** bishop and confessor (of Capua) all but Arundel, BLAdd.30511, 38624, Gough.lit.1	nothing
31 Oct	**Quentin**	**Quentin** missing from CAdd.2602
3 Nov	**Eustace**	**Wenefrid** in Harley 2785, also added to CAdd.2602; Laud. misc.299.
7 Nov	**Willebrord**; not in Arundel	nothing
10 Nov	**Martin pope**; not in Arundel	nothing
14 Nov	nothing	nothing
18 Nov	**Oct. Martin (bishop)**	**Oct. Martin**
1 Dec	**Crisanthus and Daria**; added to Rawl.C.553	nothing
4 Dec	**Barbara** (only in Sion, XVI.O.23 (added); and Cosin)	**Osmund** added to CAdd.2602, Laud. misc.299, but not to Sanctorale

Although there is a distinct set of saints present in the York books (see table of differences), some do not appear in every source. Bold York feastdays in this list appear in every MS with York responsory series that is complete at the relevant point.

York only:

Dep. Edward confessor; Transl. William; Paul hermit; Remigius (on 13 Jan; with Hilary); **Antony**; Germanicus; Emerenciana; Babillus; **Polycarp**; **Gilbert**; **Albinus**; **Transl. Wilfrid**; Sytha; Theodore; **Urban**; Bede; **Petroc**; **William**; **Oct. William**; Botulph; **Leufrid**; **Grimbald**; **Everild**; Martha; Hilda; **Aidan**; Evurtius; Maurillus; Pelagia; **Paulinus**; **Wilfrid**; **Relics** (York); **Austreberta**; Germanus; Eustace; Willebrord; Martin pope; Crisanthus and Daria; Barbara.

Sarum only:

Oct. Thomas; Lucian; Sulpicius; David; Felix bishop; Patrick; Richard; Transl. Edmund king and martyr; Dep. Erkenwald; Transl. Nicholas; Aldhelm; Medard/ Gildard; Transl. Richard; Relics (Sarum); Transl. Osmund; 7 Brothers; Dominic; Timothy/Apollinaris; Cuthberga; Ordinatio St Gregory; Edith; Gereon; Michael in monte tumba; Etheldreda; Frideswide; Wenefrid; Osmund.

Table 5 – Melodic variants

Note: In the course of this project all plainchant was transcribed according to the standard for electronic formatting proposed by Andrew Hughes in Late Medieval Liturgical Offices, vol. 2 (chapter 8). Simply put, absolute pitches are not recorded. The numerical codes below represent pitches in relation to the Final of the mode, with 1 representing the Final, 2 the pitch a second above, and so on. Pitches below the final are represented by 0 (a second below); - (a third below); * (a fourth below); repercussions (two consecutive, identical pitches in the same syllable) indicated by =; pitches representing liquescents followed by a comma (thus 4,) syllable breaks are indicated by the . character: thus, the familiar ending in mode 6 with final F:

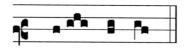

Do-   mi-nus

becomes dominus.1232.12.21.

This format is compact, amenable to rapid computer entry, and many such examples are more quickly compared than are facsimiles of square notation. Further details, and a simplified guide to plainchant, are in chapters 7 and 8 of Hughes's book.

In the tables below, details are given in abbreviated form: A2 MR6.8g could be read 'Matins responsory 6 on the second Sunday of Advent, in mode 8 with final G.' Fri MV7.6f, then, is 'Matins verse 7 on Good Friday, in mode 6 with final F.'

Variants in a single manuscript are given in footnotes.

* * *

Minor variants
Repercussion added

A2 MR6.8g	tuum	York 23=2.2; Sarum 232.2
A2 MR6.8g	gaude	York 4==.42; Sarum 4=.42
A2 MR6.8g	iacob	York 354=.3²; Sarum 3543.3³
A3 MV4.4e	gravida	York 2.1232=.21; Sarum 2.1232.21
Fri MV7.6f	astiterunt	York 1.1.124.434323=2; Sarum 1.1.124.4343232

Simple pitch inserted or omitted

A2 MR6.8g	letare	York 4.565.4; Sarum 4.565.43
A3 MR4.4e	verbum	York 23.32=1010; Sarum 23.32=010
A3 MR4.4e	paries	York 4.34.3234343212=1; Sarum 4.34.323434312=1
A3 MR4.4e	benedicta	York 21.2.3.2; Sarum 021.2.3.2
A3 MR4.4e	domino	York 3434.212101.10; Sarum 3434.3212101
A3 MR4.4e	verbum	York 23.32=1010; Sarum 23.32=010
A3 MV4.4e	detrimentum	York 34.32.12.10; Sarum 34.3.12.10
A3 MV4.4e	filium	York 45.4.3; Sarum 45.43.3
Fri MR7.6f	sicut	York 121.23; Sarum 121.232
Fri MR7.6f	gigantes	York 35.21,.1201-*-0-; Sarum 345.21,.1201-*-0- ⁴
Fri MV7.6f	unum	York 423432.232121; Sarum 42432.23212=1

² Sion: second syllable 43
³ except Laud.misc.299, which has the York version
⁴ except Laud.misc.299, which has the York version, and Sion, which has no 1
  iquescent 1, on 2nd syllable

Major variants

| A1 MR1.7g | dicite | York | 54.564.45()7676565 |
| | | Sarum | 54.564.4567675676 |

York has 1 fewer pitch, last 4 pitches have different contour

| A1 MR1.7g | israel | York | 2.14.4=343465342... |
| | | Sarum | 1.24.4=343465432... |

exchange across sylls 1, 2

| A1 MR1.7g | regnaturus | York | 1.24.4().54343232 |
| | | Sarum | 1.24.43.54=32 |

York has 1 fewer pitch, and has 4 pitches instead of repercussion.

| A2 MR6.8g | convertere | York | 1.2.1.0 |
| | | Sarum | 12.2.12101.10 |

York simple, syllabic; Sarum more florid, melismatic

| A2 MR6.8g | exaltabis | York | 1.24.43454324.121 |
| | | Sarum | 1.24.434523.21 |

indescribable; both end ...21

| A3 MR4.4e | angelum | York | 2.34.4523 |
| | | Sarum | 2.43.4=23 |

exchange on second syllable; one pitch changes by a 2nd

| A3 MR4.4e | concipies | York | 4.45.4.43=1[5] |
| | | Sarum | 45.4.4.43=1 |

exchange of 1st and 2nd sylls.

| A3 MV4.4e | efficieris | York | 02.45.4.34.32[6] |
| | | Sarum | ()2.34.32.34.32 |

York has additional pitch; 2nd and 3rd sylls different

| Fri MR7.6f | fortes | York | -0(   )-=*,.-* |
| | | Sarum | -010-0-=*,.-* |

Sarum 4 pitches longer

| Fri MR7.6f | pepercerunt | York | 4.32,.42=12.21 |
| | | Sarum | 4.3=2.42343212.21 |

Sarum has extra repercussion and additional pitches replacing York reperc'n.

---

[5] Arundel: first syllable is 43,.

[6] YAdd69 has last two syllables 34.21

BIBLIOGRAPHY

Manuscript sources

Note: Unless otherwise cited all comments here are based on observation; fuller information may be found in the relevant catalogues, for which citations are given if available.

Arundel Castle Archives
- MS s. n. (the 'York Antiphonal')

Antiphonal, for the collegiate chapel of St Mary and the Holy Angels, York Minster (engraving on boards, and cursive inscription on f. 2v). Temporale f. 3r; Sanctorale f. 156r, ending f. 257v, with commemoration of all Saints. No Calendar, Psalter, or Litany.

Notes: Frere, Morgan, and Hughes list this Antiphonal at Everingham Park in the library of Lord Herries in addition to a MS at Arundel – only one exists. This manuscript was removed to Arundel Castle Archives after the Herries title was assumed by the Fitzalan-Howards.

Not in Bibliotheca norfolciana: a catalogue of selected manuscripts and printed books in the library of His Grace the Duke of Norfolk (1961).

Cambridge University Library
- MS Additional 2602

Antiphonal (Sarum), for Springfield church, Essex. Temporale f. 1r; Calendar f. 125r; Psalter f. 131. Litany f. 166r; Sanctorale f. 179r. Common f. 283v.

Notes: A brief account of the discovery of this MS is pasted on modern endpapers; it was hidden at the Reformation in the church and recovered in the 19th century.

- MS Additional 3110

Breviary, unknown origin, province of York. Temporale f. 17r (Leaves 1–16 gone). Psalter: much lacking, from f. 153; 161–216 gone. No Calendar. Sanctorale f. 217r. No Litany. All Saints: f. 315v; Dead f. 318r. Common f. 333r.

Notes: many modern annotations in pencil, especially the word 'Northern', on feasts of 'York saints'.

Durham University Library [Palace Green]
- MS Cosin V.I.2

Noted breviary, for Rudby parish church. Temporale begins imperfectly on the first Sunday after the octave of Pentecost, f. 1r. Calendar f. 23r. Psalter f. 26r. Litany f. 46r. Sanctorale begins incomplete ff. 61–106v (end)
Notes: detailed notes by Ian Doyle available locally.

LONDON, BRITISH LIBRARY
- MS Additional 30511
Breviary, unknown origin, province of York. No Temporale; Calendar f. 8r; Psalter f. 14r; additional material including office for William between fols. 99–107; Common f. 108r; Sanctorale f. 128v.

- MS Additional 34190 / Egerton 2025
Breviary, unknown origin, province of York. Addl. 34190 and Egerton ms 2025 contain fragments of the same manuscript, including a Calendar, partial Temporale, partial Psalter and Litany, and partial Sanctorale. The Egerton ms contains the Calendar and Sunday of Advent 4, from which data were taken.

- MS Additional 38624
Breviary, unknown origin, province of York. Begins mid-Psalter f. 1; Litany f. 15. Common and Sanctorale with contents mixed and out of order, f. 19, beginning with SS Tiburtius and Valerian and ending with All Saints and the Common of several Virgins.

- MS Burney 335
Breviary, Cistercian. Calendar f. 1r; Psalter f. 7r; Litany f. 63r followed by Temporale; Sanctorale f. 200r. All Saints f. 288r; no Dead; Common f. 305r.
Notes: Not a secular York manuscript. Hughes suggests Norwich or 'northern England'.

- MS Harley 2785
Breviary (Sarum). Temporale f. 1r; Calendar f. 170r; Psalter f. 176r, Litany f. 214r; Common, f. 237r. Sanctorale f. 259r, imperfect, ending with Barnabas (June).
Notes: Additions for the Conception and Margaret precede the Common.

LONDON, LAMBETH PALACE LIBRARY
- MS Sion College 1 (olim Sion College MS Arc.L.40.2/L.1)
Noted breviary, for Skelton parish church.
See the facsimile with commentary by Hughes.

NOTTINGHAM UNIVERSITY LIBRARY [KING'S MEADOW]
- MS s.n., the 'Wollaton Antiphonal'

Antiphonal (Sarum), used at St Leonard's church, Wollaton.
Notes: Complete but unbound and in gatherings, but most are unavailable
for consultation. The first gathering (ff.1–8) is unavailable; Advent
continues in gatherings 2-4 (ff. 9–32); the Triduum begins f. 122. All
remaining parts of this manuscript have not been seen.

OXFORD, BODLEIAN LIBRARY
- MS Bodley 68 (SC 2142)

Astronomical calendar 'to which the principal feasts have been added'.
Calendar f. 39v.
See van Dijk III 136.

- MS e Musaeo 126 (SC 3612)

Processional, province of York. Litanies from ff. 40v, 44v, and 57v.
See van Dijk V 60, 200.

- MS Gough liturg. 1, olim Gough Missals 36. (SC 18328)

Noted breviary (incomplete), province of York. No Temporale or Kalendar;
Psalter f. 7r imperfect, beginning at Ps 66.11; Common f. 31r; Sanctorale f.
54r, imperfect.
See van Dijk II 229.

- MS Gough liturg. 5 (SC 18341)

Manual, province of York (marginal note: 'Manuale Secundum Usum
Ebor – vide ad finem libri'. At the back is written in the main hand 'explicit
manuale scd'm usum ebor') Litany begins at virgins, f. 1r; another Litany
for procession from f. 22r. Office for the Dead with complete antiphons and
psalms first for Matins at f. 29r; lessons and responsories begin f. 34v, but
end at f. 36r.
See van Dijk III 48.

- MS Lat. liturg. f. 2 (SC 29741)

Hours (Sarum) Select MS; seen on film only (Bodleian reel SFW.104).
Litany f. 75v. Dead f. 80r, corresponding with Sarum pattern.
See van Dijk IV–B 145.

- MS Laud misc. 84 (SC 1219)

Breviary, perhaps York Minster. Temporale f. 1r; Calendar f. 163r; Litany f.
211r; Common f. 220; Sanctorale f. 242; Dead f. 368v.
See van Dijk II 254.

- MS Laud misc. 299 (SC 752)

Breviary (Sarum), for Launton parish church. Temporale f. 1r; Calendar f. 229r; Psalter f. 235; Dead f. 273r; Common f. 277r; Sanctorale f. 305. See van Dijk II 233.

- MS Liturg. 132 (SC 30608)

Hours, unknown origin. Calendar f. 13r, including John of Beverley, William, Paulinus. No office for the Dead.

Notes: Described by van Dijk (IV 147) as a Sarum book for the diocese of York, perhaps by a Netherlandish scribe.

- MS Rawlinson C. 553 (SC 12399)

Hours, possibly for St Mary's, York. Calendar, f. 7r; Litany f. 120r; Dead f. 134r. Calendar monastic but 'made into a secular one' (van Dijk, IV–A 7). Office for the Dead modified, may have originally followed Sarum order, but corrected to York order.

- MS Rawlinson G. 170 (SC 14893)

Psalter, written for the province of York. Calendar f. 2r; Litany f. 212v; Dead f. 220v.

See van Dijk II 54

- MS Wood C. 12 (SC 8571)

Hours (Sarum), perhaps for Beverley. Calendar f. 1; Litany f. 171r; Dead f. 184r.

Notes: Tentatively attributed to Beverley by van Dijk on the strength of 'two feasts of St John of Beverley' in the calendar (van Dijk, IV 175)

York Minster Library

- MS XVI. O. 9

Missal-breviary, for the province of York. Temporale f. 1r; Calendar f. 118r; Psalter f. 124r; Litany f. 163v, Prefaces, canon, and proper prayers for masses f. 169v; Sanctorale f. 188r; Common f. 257r.

- MS XVI. O. 23

Breviary (summer volume only), for the province of York. Temporale f. 1r, beginning with vigil of Easter; Calendar f. 141r; Psalter f. 147r; Litany f. 245r; Sanctorale f. 249r, beginning with Ambrose. 1 leaf missing before Common, f. 429.

- MS Additional 68

Breviary, for the province of York. Calendar f. 147r; Psalter f. 153r; Litany f. 221r; New signature at f. 223, with offices for Edward confessor,

Translation of Wilfrid, Octave of William, Everild, Anne, Martha, Thomas of Hereford, Translation of Edward confessor, Nativity of the BVM, Vigil of Simon and Jude. Sanctorale f. 235r; Common f. 354r.

- MS Additional 69
Noted breviary, for the province of York. Temporale f. 1r; Calendar f. 150r; Psalter f. 156r; Litany f. 179r; Common f. 180r; Sanctorale f. 202r.
Notes: In extremely poor condition.

- MS Additional 70
Breviary, for Harewood church near Leeds (Ker, based on annotations and dedication added to Calendar). Temporale f. 1r; Calendar f. 160r; Psalter f. 163r; Litany f. 198v; Common f. 201r; Sanctorale f. 215r.
Notes: Offices for William and Paulinus cut out.

- MS Additional 115
Breviary, for the province of York. Temporale f. 1r; Calendar f. 141r; Psalter f. 147r; Litany f. 213r; Common f. 215v; missing leaf between 231v and 232; Sanctorale f. 232r.

- MS Additional 383
Breviary, for the province of York. Temporale f. 1r; Calendar f. 154r; Psalter f. 160r; Litany f. 220v; Sanctorale f. 235r; Common f. 352r.

Manuscript sources – facsimiles

Aberdeen, University Library
- MS 25, the 'Burnet Psalter'
Psalter/Hours, digitized with indexed facsimiles available at http://www.abdn.ac.uk/diss/historic/collects/bps/bpcontents.htm.

Printed works

Aylmer, G.E., and Reginald Cant, eds. *A History of York Minster* (Oxford, 1977).

Backhouse, Janet, ed. *The Madresfield Hours. A fourteenth-century manuscript in the library of Earl Beauchamp*, Roxburghe Club (Oxford, 1975).

Barrow, Julia, ed. *English Episcopal Acta. Hereford 1079–1234*. (Oxford, 1993).

Baumstark, Anton, *Comparative Liturgy*, tr. F.L. Cross (London, 1958).

Baxter, Philip. *Sarum use. The development of a medieval code of liturgy and customs*. (Salisbury Cathedral, 1994).

Bishop, Edmund. 'Holy Week Rites of Sarum, Hereford, and Rouen Compared', in *Liturgica historica: papers on the liturgy and religious life of the Western Church* (Oxford, 1918)

Bergeron, Katherine, *Decadent Enchantments: the revival of Gregorian chant at Solesmes* (Berkeley, 1998).

The boke of the common praier and administration of the Sacraments… (Worcester: Ioannis Osweni, 1549) STC 16271. Accessed through Early English Books Online.

Bowers, Roger, 'Taverner, John' in Stanley Sadie, ed., *The New Grove Dictionary of Music and Musicians* (London, 2001), vol. 18, 600.

Bradshaw, Henry, and Christopher Wordsworth, eds. *Statutes of Lincoln Cathedral with illustrative documents* (Cambridge, 1897).

Bradshaw, Paul, *The Search for the Origins of Christian Worship* (London, 1992).

Catto, Jeremy, 'Religious Change under Henry V', in G.L. Harriss, ed., *Henry V: The Practice of Kingship* (Oxford, 1985).

Colton, Lisa, 'Music in pre-Reformation York: a new source and some thoughts on the York Masses', *Plainsong and Medieval Music* 12 (2003), 71–88.

Dondi, Cristina, *The Liturgy of the Canons Regular of the Holy Sepulchre of Jerusalem. A Study and a Catalogue of the Manuscript Sources*, Bibliotheca Victorina 16 (Brepols, 2004)

Duff, E. Gordon, *A Century of the English Book Trade. Short notices of all printers, stationers, book-binders, and others …* (London, 1948).

Edwards, Owain Tudor, 'How many Sarum Antiphonals were there in England in the middle of the sixteenth century?', *Revue Bénédictine* 99 (1989), 155–80.

Farmer, David, *The Oxford Dictionary of Saints*, 5th ed (Oxford, 2004).

Frere, Walter Howard, 'The Connexion between English and Norman Rites', in J.H. Arnold and E.G.P. Wyatt, eds, *Walter Howard Frere. A Collection of his Papers on Liturgical and Historical Subjects*, Alcuin Club Collections 35 (Oxford, 1940).

—, Bibliotheca musico-liturgica. *A descriptive hand list of the musical and Latin-liturgical MSS. of the Middle Ages, preserved in the libraries of Great Britain and Ireland*, 2 vols (London, 1894–1932).

—, *Graduale Sarisburiense. A reproduction in facsimile of a manuscript of the thirteenth century, with a dissertation and historical index illustrating its development from the Gregorian Antiphonale Monasticum*, Plainsong and Medieval Music Society (Farnborough, 1966).

— and Langton E.G. Brown, eds, *The Hereford Breviary, edited from the Rouen edition of 1505*, 3 vols (London, 1904–1915).

—, 'The Use of Exeter' in J.H. Arnold and E.G.P. Wyatt, eds, *Walter Howard Frere. A Collection of his Papers on Liturgical and Historical Subjects*. Alcuin Club Collections 35 (Oxford, 1940), 54-71.

—, *The Use of Sarum. The original texts edited from the mss*, 2 vols (Cambridge, 1898–1901).

—, 'York Service Books' in J.H. Arnold and E.G.P. Wyatt, eds, *Walter Howard Frere. A Collection of his Papers on Liturgical and Historical Subjects*. Alcuin Club Collections 35 (Oxford, 1940), 159–169.

Gy, Pierre-Marie. 'Les repons de matines des trois nuits avant Pâques et la géographie liturgique du moyen age latin' in Daniel Saulnier, ed., *Requirentes modos musicos. Mélanges offerts à Dom Jean Claire* (Solesmes, 1995), 29–39.

Haines, R. M., 'Canterbury versus York: Fluctuating Fortunes in a Perennial Conflict', in *Ecclesia Anglicana: Studies in the English Church of the Later Middle Ages* (Toronto, 1989), pp. 69–105.

Harper, John, *The Forms and Order of Western Liturgy from the Tenth to the Eighteenth Centuries* (Oxford, 1991).

Henderson, W.G., *Missale ad usum insignis ecclesie Eboracensis*, Surtees Society 59–60 (London, 1874).

Hesbert, René-Jean, *Corpus antiphonalium officii*, 6 vols, Rerum Ecclesiasticarum Documenta, series maior 7–12 (Rome, 1963–79).

Heslop, T.A., 'The Canterbury calendars and the Norman Conquest', in Richard Eales and Richard Sharpe, eds, *Canterbury and the Norman conquest. Churches, saints and scholars 1066–1199* (London, 1995), 52–83.

Hiley, David, 'The Norman chant traditions – Normandy, Britain, Sicily', *Proceedings of the Royal Musical Association* 107 (1980-81), 1–33.

—, 'Writings on Western Plainchant in the 1980s and 1990s', *Acta Musicologica* 69, fasc. 1 (1997), pp. 53–93.

Hugh the Chanter, *The History of the Church of York, 1066–1127*, ed. and tr. C. Johnson, revd M. Brett and C.N.L. Brooke, Oxford Medieval Texts (Oxford, 1990).

Hughes, Andrew, *Late Medieval Liturgical Offices*, 2 vols, (Toronto, 1994–1996).

—, ed., *Lambeth Palace Sion College ms L1. The noted breviary of York*, 2 vols (Ottawa, 2000)

—, *Medieval Manuscripts for Mass and Office. A guide to their organization and terminology* (Toronto, 1982).

James, M. R., *A Catalogue of the Medieval Manuscripts in the University Library Aberdeen* (Cambridge, 1932).

Jankulak, Karen, *The Medieval Cult of St Petroc* (Woodbridge, 2000).

John of Glastonbury, *Chronica sive Historia de Rebus Glastoniensibus, ed. Thomas Hearne* (Oxford, 1726).

Ker. N. R., *Medieval Libraries of Great Britain. A list of surviving books*, 2nd edn (London, 1964).

—, and A.J. Piper, *Medieval Manuscripts in British Libraries*, 5 vols (Oxford, 1969–2002).

King, Pamela M., *The York Mystery Cycle and the Worship of the City* (Cambridge, 2006).

Lawley, S.W., *Breviarium ad usum insignis ecclesie Eboracensis*, Surtees Society 71, 75 (1880–82).

Legg, John Wickham, *The Sarum Missal, edited from three early manuscripts* (Oxford, 1916)

Le Roux, Raymond, 'Répons du Triduo Sacro et de Pâques', *Etudes Gregoriennes* 18 (1979), 157–176.

Lingard, John, *The Antiquities of the Anglo-Saxon Church*, 2nd edn (London, 1810).

Maskell, William, *The Ancient Liturgy of the Church of England, according to the uses of Sarum, York, Hereford, and Bangor* (Oxford, 1882).

Morgan, Nigel, 'The Introduction of the Sarum Calendar into the Dioceses of England in the Thirteenth Century', in Michael Prestwich et al., eds, *Thirteenth Century England VII Proceedings of the Durham Conference 1999* (Woodbridge, 2001), 179–206.

Norton, Christopher, *Archbishop Thomas of Bayeux and the Norman Cathedral at York*, Borthwick Paper 100 (York, 2001).

—, *St William of York* (Woodbridge, 2006).

Ortenberg, Veronica, *The English Church and the Continent in the Tenth and Eleventh Centuries. Cultural, Spiritual, and Artistic Exchanges* (Oxford, 1992).

Ottosen, Knud, *L'antiphonaire latin au moyen-age : réorganisation des séries de répons de l'Avent classés par R.-J. Hesbert* (Rome, 1986).

—, *The responsories and versicles of the Latin Office of the Dead* (Aarhus, Denmark, 1993).

Padel, O.J., 'Local saints and place-names in Cornwall', in Alan Thacker and Richard Sharpe, eds, *Local Saints and Local Churches in the Early Medieval West* (Oxford, 2002), 303–60.

Pfaff, Richard W., *Liturgical Calendars, Saints, and Services in Medieval England* (Aldershot, 1998).

—, *New Liturgical Feasts in Later Medieval England*, (Oxford, 1970).

Powicke, F.M., and C. R. Cheney, eds, *Councils & Synods, with other documents relating to the English church*. 3 vols. (Oxford, 1964–1997).

Procter, Francis, and Christopher Wordsworth, eds, *Breviarium ad usum insignis ecclesiae Sarum*, 3 vols (Cambridge, 1879–86).

Raine, James, ed., *The Historians of the Church of York and its Archbishops, Rerum Britannicarum medii aevi scriptores* 71, 3 vols (London, 1879–1894).

Reames, S.L., 'The Office for Saint Cecilia', in T.J. Heffernan and E.A. Matter, eds, *The Liturgy of the Medieval Church* (Kalamazoo, 2001), 349–68.

Rubenstein, Jay, 'Liturgy against history: the competing visions of Lanfranc and Eadmer of Canterbury', *Speculum* 74 (1999), 279–309.

Salisbury, Matthew. 'A 'trivial' variant: filled thirds in the office for St Thomas Becket' *Plainsong and Medieval Music* 16 no 1 (April 2007), 1–17.

Sandon, Nicholas. 'Use of Salisbury' in Stanley Sadie, ed., *The New Grove Dictionary of Music and Musicians* (London, 2001), vol. 22, 158–163.

Slocum, Kay Brainerd, *Liturgies in honour of Thomas Becket* (Toronto, 2004).

Underwood, Peter, 'Melodic traditions in medieval English antiphoners' *Journal of the Plainsong and Medieval Music Society* 5 (1982), 1–11.

William of Malmesbury, *Gesta pontificum Anglorum*, ed. and tr. M. Winterbottom, Oxford Medieval Texts (Oxford, 2007).

Wordsworth, Christopher, *Horae Eboracenses: The Prymer or hours of the Blessed Virgin Mary according to the use of the illustrious church of York*, Surtees Society 132 (1920).

Wormald, Francis, 'The Calendar of the Augustinian Priory of Launceston in Cornwall', *The Journal of Theological Studies* 39 (1938), 1–21.

—, *English Benedictine Calendars after AD 1100*, 2 vols, Henry Bradshaw Society 77, 81 (London, 1939–46).

Wilson, Susan E., *The Life and After-Life of St John of Beverley. The Evolution of the Cult of an Anglo-Saxon Saint* (Aldershot, 2006).

Unpublished works

Chadd, David, 'Beyond the Frontiers: Guides for Uncharted Territory', delivered at Frontiers of Research in Medieval Music, Dartmouth College, USA, summer 1988 (revised typescript dated October 1999).

Droste, D.L., 'The Musical Notation and Transmission of the Music of the Sarum Use, 1225–1250'. PhD dissertation, University of Toronto, 1982.

Frere, Walter Howard. Notes on Cambridge Additional 2602 (kept with the MS)

Hughes, Andrew, Heather Robbins and Matthew Salisbury, 'Cataloguing Discrepancies: the printed York Breviary of 1493'. Under review by University of Toronto Press. Provided by the authors.

Ker, N. R. Card-index for Medieval Libraries of Great Britain.

Morgan, Nigel. Database of British liturgical manuscripts sorted by use. Unpublished database. Provided by the author.

Pfaff, Richard W., 'New liturgical observances in later medieval England'. DPhil dissertation, University of Oxford, 1965.

Thomas, Islwyn Geoffrey. 'The Cult of Saints' Relics in Medieval England'. PhD dissertation, University of London, 1975.

van Dijk, S.J.P., Handlist of the Latin Liturgical Manuscripts in the Bodleian Library Oxford, 7 vols in 8, unpublished typescript, (dated 1957–60).

Notes

1   *The boke of the common praier and administration of the Sacraments...* (1549) STC 16271.
2   D. Chadd, 'Beyond the Frontiers: Guides for Uncharted Territory'. Unpublished text (dated October 1999).
3   N. Morgan, 'The Introduction of the Sarum Calendar into the Dioceses of England in the Thirteenth Century', *Thirteenth-Century England* 8 (2001), 180–81.
4   R.W. Pfaff, *Liturgical Calendars, Saints, and Services in Medieval England* (Aldershot, 1998), 13
5   S. W. Lawley, *Breviarium ad usum insignis ecclesie Eboracensis.* Surtees Society 71, 75 (Durham, 1880–82) The 1493 York Breviary (STC 15856) was printed by Johannes Hertzog in Venice for Frederick Egmont and Gerard Barrevelt.
6   N.R. Ker and A.J. Piper, *Medieval Manuscripts in British Libraries.* 5 vols (Oxford, 1969–2002) iv, 816 (on York Minster Add. 69)
7   Sherry Reames's article on the office for St Cecilia is among a number of studies forced to rely on the edition. See 'The Office for Saint Cecilia' in T.J. Heffernan and E.A. Matter, eds., *The Liturgy of the Medieval Church* (Kalamazoo, 2001), 260.
8   See especially John Wickham Legg's *Sarum Missal* (Oxford, 1916), particularly pp. xiii–iv, and Walter Howard Frere's *Graduale Sarisburiense... illustrating its development from the Gregorian Antiphonale...* (Farnborough, 1966).
9   P. Bradshaw, *The Search for the Origins of Christian Worship* (London, 1992), ix.
10 F. Procter and C. Wordsworth, eds. *Breviarium... Sarum.* (Cambridge, 1879–86), vol. 2, vii.
11 Pfaff *Liturgical Calendars*, 204.
12 Ibid, 1; especially those that deal with minutiae.
13 *Sarum Use: the development of a medieval code of liturgy and customs* (Salisbury Cathedral, 1994), 8, 32.
14 which may explain the interest in it – ibid., 78.
15 A.S. Duncan-Jones, in J.H. Arnold and E.G.P. Wyatt, *Walter Howard Frere: a collection of his papers on liturgical and historical subjects* (London, 1940), xi.
16 A. Baumstark, *Comparative Liturgy* (London, 1958), 3.
17 R-J Hesbert, *Corpus Antiphonalium Officii* (6 vols), Rerum Ecclesiasticarum Documenta 7–12 (Rome, 1963–79).
18 Hesbert, preface to *CAO* vol. 1.
19 D. Hiley 'Writings on Western Plainchant in the 1980s and 1990s', in *Acta Musicologica* 69, fasc. 1 (Jan-Jun 1997), 67.
20 R. le Roux, 'Répons du Triduo Sacro et de Pâques', in *Etudes Gregoriennes* 18 (1979), 157–76; P-M Gy, 'Les reponses de matines...' in D. Saulnier, ed., *Requirentes modos musicos* (Solesmes, 1995)
21 Beyssac's work is unpublished, but see K. Ottosen, *The Responsories and Versicles of the Latin Office of the Dead* (Aarhus, Denmark, 1993), 3.
22 Ottose, *Responsories*, 4.
23 J. Backhouse, ed., *The Madresfield Hours: a fourteenth-century manuscript in the library of Earl Beauchamp.* Roxburghe Club (Oxford, 1975), 6. She also mentions their translation feasts and material for Cuthbert, Oswald, and Aidan.
24 A. Hughes, H. Robbins, and M. Salisbury, *Cataloguing Discrepancies: the printed York Breviary of 1493* (Toronto, in press).
25 I thank Nigel Morgan for supplying an unpublished handlist of York manuscripts for consultation.

26 York Minster Historical Tracts, no 19, 1927 republished in J.H. Arnold and E.G.P. Wyatt, eds., *Walter Howard Frere: a Collection of his Papers on Liturgical and Historical Subjects.* Alcuin Club Collections 35 (Oxford, 1940), pp. 167–9. It seems that he had also identified a number of sequence-hymns that were characteristic of York; notes to this effect are preserved at Cambridge in an envelope stored with CAdd.2602.

27 S.J.P. van Dijk, *Handlist of the Latin Liturgical Manuscripts in the Bodleian Library Oxford,* 7 vols. in 8, 1957–60. Typescript.

28 Droste proposes Ely. See *The Musical Notation and Transmission of the Music of the Sarum Use, 1225–1250,* (PhD dissertation, University of Toronto, 1992), 367.

29 The number of responsory series in towns in Normandy may be an example; see the lists in Ottosen, *L'antiphonaire Latin au Moyen-Age : réorganisation des séries de répons de l'Avent classés par R.-J. Hesbert,* (Rome, 1986).

30 See alphabetical index of sources, CAO vol V.

31 There are two deviations, each affecting a single item in a single source.

32 Assigned to Sarum on the basis of erased series for the Dead and other evidence; see p. 25.

33 The responsory series in this Sarum group also correspond to the Sarum series derived, insofar as they can be, from W. H. Frere's edition of the Sarum Ordinal. See *The Use of Sarum*, vol. ii, 9, for Advent 1; ii 146 for the Dead.

34 Isa 1.1–2, appending Is 45.22.

35 A1–ML6, A3–ML6, A4–ML9, Thu–ML5, Thu–ML9, Fri–ML5, Fri–ML6, Sat–ML8, Sat–ML9

36 A1–ML3, A3–ML3, A4–ML2, A4–ML3, Thu–ML6, Thu–ML8, Fri–ML2

37 A1–ML9, A2–ML2, A2–ML3, Adv2–ML4

38 Ker *MMBL*, iv, 818.

39 Ibid., iv, 820.

40 Ottosen, *Responsories*, 93.

41 Ker in *Medieval Libraries* used liturgical evidence (secondhand in many identifiable cases, based on the card-index in Duke Humfrey) to determine provenance, but the most frequent means of attribution based on this evidence was the existence of a dedication feast, probably a reliable method.

42 F. Wormald, *English Benedictine Kalendars after A.D. 1100.* 2 vols, Henry Bradshaw Society 77, 81 (London, 1939–46).

43 Morgan, 'Introduction of the Sarum Calendar', 181.

44 W.H. Frere and Langton E.G. Brown, eds. *The Hereford Breviary: edited from the Rouen edition of 1505* (London, 1904–1915), vol iii, p. xxxi. Frere, too, falls into the trap of believing that contents are uniform.

45 Pfaff *New liturgical feasts in later medieval England* (Oxford, 1970), 1, 3, 11–12.

46 Pfaff 'The Study of Medieval Liturgy' in *Liturgical Calendars*, 7.

47 Gilbert's order spread into Yorkshire; Aidan was first bishop of Lindisfarne.

48 D.H. Farmer, *The Oxford Dictionary of Saints*, 5th ed (Oxford, 2004), 188.

49 Despite Petroc's reputation as the premier saint of Cornwall Karen Jankulak reports local liturgical commemorations in Somerset, Dorset, Hampshire, Wiltshire, Oxfordshire, and London, in addition to Yorkshire. The saint did not appear in the Sarum breviary. See *The Medieval Cult of St Petroc* (Woodbridge, 2000), 209–216.

50 W.G. Henderson, *Missale ad usum insignis ecclesie Eboracensis.* Surtees Society 59–60 (London, 1874), I, xix – referring to MS A., 'Dr Gott's missal'.

51 in this case, Wormald *Calendars* 15-30, 77.

52 Wormald's source here is the *Chronica* of John of Glastonbury, which listed relics of Paulinus and the bones of Aidan among a substantial list of relics of saints in the possession of the abbey (*Chronica*, 17).

53 A good starting point may be to determine where relics of the saints were kept; ample data for this is in I.G. Thomas, *The Cult of Saints' Relics in Medieval England* (University of London PhD thesis, 1975).

54 A similar feast at Salisbury took place on the Sunday following the translation feast of Thomas Becket, and local feasts of relics were not unheard of: see note 109. Thomas (supra, 128) suggests relic feasts were often 'offshoots' of local saints' days.

55 for instance, Henderson, *Missale Eboracensis*.

56 van Dijk, IV 175. Comparison of responsory series had not emerged by the time of his catalogue.

57 see *Ecclesiastical History.* II, chp. xix.

58 S. Wilson, *The Life and After-Life of St John of Beverley. The Evolution of the Cult of an Anglo-Saxon Saint.* (Aldershot, 2006), 3, citing Wormald's *English Benedictine Kalendars.*

59 Wilson, 109.

60 C. Norton, *St William of York* (York, 2006), 202.

61 William's main feastday appears in the rather sparse Burnet calendar (f. 5v), along with Richard, Etheldreda, and Erkenwald (none of which are found in any York MS). He is the last of the confessors in the Litany (f. 244r). Memorials to John of Beverley and to William appear in the Office of the BVM (ff. 259v–60r). The antiphon for William *O Willelme pastor bone* recalls a votive antiphon prescribed in the statutes of Cardinal College, Oxford (i.e. the *Collegium Thomae Wolsey Cardinalis Eboracensis*). (For the votive antiphon, see Roger Bowers, *Taverner, John* in Stanley Sadie, ed., *The New Grove Dictionary of Music and Musicians*, vol. 18, 600. I thank Lisa Colton for this recollection.) Despite William and John, M.R. James links the Burnet MS to Ely, based on material for Etheldreda. See James, *A Catalogue of the Medieval Manuscripts in the University Library Aberdeen* (Cambridge, 1932), 30. My survey of the office of the Dead (f. 273ff) indicates a Sarum responsory series. For the Cornish calendar, in which William appears with Paulinus, see Francis Wormald, 'The Calendar of the Augustinian Priory of Launceston in Cornwall', *The Journal of Theological Studies* 39 (1938), 4.

62 XVI.O.9, Add.69, Add.30511

63 3: XVI.O.9, EArC, Gough.lit.1; 9: YAdd.115, BLAdd.30511, BLAdd.38624. Normally six proper lessons are given.

64 van Dijk, IV–A, 7.

65 Cuthbert, John, Wilfrid, William, Botulph.

66 The additions to the calendar are done in textualis script resembling (or made to resemble) the original hand, while the notes are in a more casual cursive.

67 Prisca, Germanicus, German, Petroc, Botulph, Leufrid, Grimbald, Praxedis, Aidan, Tecla, Francis, Austreberta, pope Martin.

68 T.A. Heslop, 'The Canterbury calendars and the Norman Conquest' in Richard Eales and Richard Sharpe, eds. *Canterbury and the Norman conquest: churches, saints and scholars 1066–1199* (London, 1995), 72–77.

69 Square notation had been included in German and Italian printed books from about 1475, but in English books it did remain quite rare. See Martin Picker, 'Ottaviano dei Petrucci' in S. Sadie, ed., *New Grove*, vol 14, 595.

70 D. Hiley, 'The Norman chant traditions – Normandy, Britain, Sicily' *Proceedings of the Royal*

Musical Association 107 (1980–81), 1–33; P. Underwood, 'Melodic traditions in medieval English antiphoners' *Journal of the Plainsong and Medieval Music Society* 5 (1982), 1–11.

71 a term coined by Hughes; a single word and its musical setting.

72 Trivial variants can be good indicators of local practice; see M. Salisbury, 'A 'trivial' variant: filled thirds in the office for St Thomas Becket' *Plainsong and Medieval Music* 16 (Apr 2007), 1–17.

73 Underwood, 'Melodic traditions', 2.

74 L. Colton, 'Music in pre-Reformation York: a new source and some thoughts on the York Masses' *Plainsong and Medieval Music* 12 (Apr 2003), 74.

75 C. Dondi, *The liturgy of the Canons Regular of the Holy Sepulchre of Jerusalem: a study and a catalogue of the manuscript sources* (Turnhout, 2004), 120.

76 See the relevant series in Ottosen *L'antiphonaire latin* . pp. 47–8, 120–1, 140–1, 192, 234, respectively.

77 Ottosen *Responsories*, 251, 120–1.

78 Dondi, 138.

79 We are also limited by the Normandy sources: there may yet exist series that are still undocumented in Hesbert et al that might be closer to the York pattern.

80 E. Bishop 'Holy Week Rites of Sarum, Hereford, and Rouen Compared' in *Liturgica historica: papers on the liturgy and religious life of the Western Church* (Oxford, 1918), 277.

81 R.M.T. Hill and C.N.L. Brooke, 'From 627 until the Early Thirteenth Century' in G.E. Aylmer and R. Cant, eds, *A History of York Minster* (Oxford, 1977), 27.

82 H. Bradshaw and C. Wordsworth, eds., *Statutes of Lincoln Cathedral with illustrative documents* (Cambridge, 1897) ii, pp. 824ff (hereafter LCS)

83 'Precipimus... ut festa beati Swthuni et beati Byrini, qui ecclesie et episcopatus nostri sunt patroni... et festa aliorum sanctorum, quorum corpora in ecclesia nostra vel aliis ecclesiis nostre diocesis resquiescunt, in kalendarisis scribantur, et quando contigunt denuntientur et in ecclesiis celebrentur.' Statutes of Winchester I (1224) in F.M. Powicke and C. R. Cheney, eds. *Councils & synods, with other documents relating to the English church* 3 vols. (Oxford, 1964–1997), II–i, 127.

84 LCS ii, 835 (citing Wilkins *Concilia* i 677–8.)

85 O.J. Padel 'Local saints and place-names in Cornwall', in A. Thacker and R. Sharpe, eds., *Local saints and local churches in the early medieval West* (Oxford, 2002), 338–9

86 LCS ii, 842–3, citing Wilkins *Concilia* iii 234–5.

87 *Councils and Synods,* II–i, 435

88 LCS ii, 838, citing Macray *Sarum Charters* (Rolls Series) p. 369.

89 W.H. Frere, 'The Use of Exeter' in J.H. Arnold and E.G.P. Wyatt, eds., *Walter Howard Frere: a Collection of his Papers on Liturgical and Historical Subjects*. Alcuin Club Collections no XXXV (Oxford, 1940), 57.

90 LCS ii, 838, citing *Reg Melton* 516a.

91 W.H. Frere, *The use of Sarum: the original texts edited from the mss.* 2 vols. (Cambridge, 1898–1901).

92 cf *Councils and Synods* Canterbury II–i 29; Salisbury II–i 79; Chichester II–i 460. Each takes the form 'Precepimus... quod omnes... habeant canonem misse secundum ecclesie N. correctum...'

93 LCS ii, 844, citing Dugdale *Monast.* vi., 1337.

94 Statutes of Wells, 1258 (*Councils and Synods* II–i 599, 613).

95 British Library Lansdowne 397 f. 245r

96 LCS ii, 123–132.

97 J. Rubenstein, 'Liturgy against history: the competing visions of Lanfranc and Eadmer of Canterbury'. *Speculum* 74 (1999), 281.

98 Heslop in Eales and Sharpe, 61.

99 Ibid., 56.

100 Rubenstein, 307.

101 Pfaff *Liturgical calendars*, 106, 108.

102 Ibid., 19–20.

103 Nothing to this effect appears in *English Episcopal Acta*, vii (Hereford), except that he instituted a feast of relics at Leominster (no. 31), 31.

104 Bishop, 298.

105 Dondi, 138–9.

106 Aylmer and Cant, 19.

107 Hugh the Chanter. *The history of the Church of York, 1066–1127*, ed. and tr. Charles Johnson. Oxford Medieval Texts (Oxford, 1990), 3, also note 2. Not to mention that according to William of Malmesbury in the *Gesta Pontificum Anglorum* Thomas is described as having an interest in composing verse, and converting it to 'the mode of divine praise', surely a useful trait for a liturgical author. (iii.116*.3)

108 Hugh, 21. Emphasis mine.

109 C. Norton, *Archbishop Thomas of Bayeux and the Norman Cathedral at York* (York, 2001), 1–2.

110 E. Bishop, *Liturgica historica*, 276.

111 To give an example from the Mass books, Henderson observes that the York missal at Sidney Sussex College, Cambridge (MS 33) contained postcommunions associated with Sarum: see *Missale Eboracensis*, x.

112 I have completed an inventory of its contents, as present catalogue entries comprise one handwritten line in the library's printed catalogue. Based on these observations, the librarian of the Duke of Norfolk now agrees in principle to support digitization of the manuscript and work will soon proceed.

113 Funds will be required for its continued restoration, and sustained work required to study the manuscript.

114 Were printed York breviaries commissioned to preserve the York office from being taken over by cheap, accessible Sarum volumes? It seems unlikely at the outset: only a few editions of Sarum breviaries and missals were produced before the 1490s, and the 1493 edition was commissioned by Frederick Egmont and Gerard Barrevelt, who also commissioned a number of Sarum books. (See Duff, *A Century of the English Book Trade*, 71). However by the 1520s several editions had been commissioned by York residents. More study will be necessary to address this question.